WILLIAM THE CONQUEROR

MAKERS of HISTORY

William the Conqueror

BY

JACOB ABBOTT

MCMIV

JOHN D. MORRIS AND
COMPANY
PHILADELPHIA

PREFACE.

In selecting the subjects for the successive volumes of this series, it has been the object of the author to look for the names of those great personages whose histories constitute useful, and not merely entertaining, knowledge. There are certain names which are familiar, as names, to all mankind; and every person who seeks for any degree of mental cultivation, feels desirous of informing himself of the leading outlines of their history, that he may know, in brief, what it was in their characters or their doings which has given them so widely-extended a fame. This knowledge, which it seems incumbent on every one to obtain in respect to such personages as Hannibal, Alexander, Cæsar, Cleopatra, Darius, Xerxes, Alfred, William the Conqueror, Queen Elizabeth, and Mary Queen of Scots, it is the design and object of these volumes to communicate, in a faithful, and, at the same time, if possible, in an attractive manner. Consequently, great historical names alone are selected; and it has been the writer's aim to present the prominent and leading traits in their characters, and all the important events in their lives, in a bold and free manner, and yet in the plain and simple language which is so obviously required in works which aim at permanent and practical usefulness.

CONTENTS.

ENGRAVINGS.

WILLIAM THE CONQUEROR.

CHAPTER I.

NORMANDY.

ONE of those great events in English history, which occur at distant intervals, and
form, respectively, a sort of bound or landmark,
to which all other events, preceding or following them for centuries, are referred, is what is
called the Norman Conquest.   The Norman
Conquest was, in fact, the accession of William,
duke of Normandy, to the English throne.
This accession was not altogether a matter of
military force, for William claimed a *right* to
the throne, which, if not altogether perfect, was,
as he maintained, at any rate superior to that
of the prince against whom he contended.   The
rightfulness of his claim was, however, a matter of little consequence, except so far as the
moral influence of it aided him in gaining possession.   The right to rule was, in those days,

14   WILLIAM THE CONQUEROR.

The right of the strongest.   Map of Normandy.

rather more openly and nakedly, though not much more really, than it is now, the right of the strongest.

Normandy, William's native land, is a very rich and beautiful province in the north of France. The following map shows its situation:

Map of England and part of France, showing the situation of Normandy.

It lies, as will be seen upon the map, on the coast of France, adjoining the English Channel. The Channel is here irregular in form, but may be, perhaps, on the average, one hundred miles wide. The line of coast on the southern side of the Channel, which forms, of course, the northern border of Normandy, is a range of cliffs, which are almost perpendicular toward the sea, and which frown forbiddingly upon every ship that sails along the shore. Here and there, it is true, a river opens a passage for itself among these cliffs from the interior, and these river mouths would form harbors into which ships might enter from the offing, were it not that the northwestern winds prevail so generally, and drive such a continual swell of rolling surges in upon the shore, that they choke up all these estuary openings, as well as every natural indentation of the land, with shoals and bars of sand and shingle. The reverse is the case with the northern, or English shore of this famous channel. There the harbors formed by the mouths of the rivers, or by the sinuosities of the shore, are open and accessible, and at the same time sheltered from the winds and the sea. Thus, while the northern or English shore has been, for many centuries, all the time enticing

16   WILLIAM THE CONQUEROR.

Nature of the English coast.   Northmen and Danes

the seaman in and out over the calm, deep, and
sheltered waters which there penetrate the land,
the southern side has been an almost impassa-
ble barrier, consisting of a long line of frowning
cliffs, with every opening through it choked with
shoals and sand-banks, and guarded by the rolling and tumbling of surges which scarcely ever
rest.

It is in a great measure owing to these great
physical differences between the two shores,
that the people who live upon the one side,
though of the same stock and origin with those
who live upon the other, have become so vastly
superior to them in respect to naval exploits and
power.   They are really of the same stock and
origin, since both England and the northern
part of France were overrun and settled by
what is called the Scandinavian race, that is,
people from Norway, Denmark, and other countries on the Baltic.   These people were called
the *Northmen* in the histories of those times.
Those who landed in England are generally
termed *Danes*, though but a small portion of
them came really from Denmark.   They were
all, however, of the same parent stock, and possessed the same qualities of courage, energy,
and fearless love of adventure and of danger

which distinguish their descendants at the present day. They came down in those early times in great military hordes, and in fleets of piratical ships, through the German Ocean and the various British seas, braving every hardship and every imaginable danger, to find new regions to dwell in, more genial, and fertile, and rich than their own native northern climes. In these days they evince the same energy, and endure equal privations and hardships, in hunting whales in the Pacific Ocean; in overrunning India, and seizing its sources of wealth and power; or in sallying forth, whole fleets of adventurers at a time, to go more than half round the globe, to dig for gold in California. The times and circumstances have changed, but the race and spirit are the same.

Normandy takes its name from the Northmen. It was the province of France which the Northmen made peculiarly their own. They gained access to it from the sea by the River Seine, which, as will be seen from the map, flows, as it were, through the heart of the country. The lower part of this river, and the sea around its mouth, are much choked up with sand and gravel, which the waves have been for ages washing in. Their incessant industry

28—2

would result in closing up the passage entirely,
were it not that the waters of the river must
have an outlet; and thus the current, setting
outward, wages perpetual war with the surf
and surges which are continually breaking in.
The expeditions of the Northmen, however,
found their way through all these obstructions.
They ascended the river with their ships, and
finally gained a permanent settlement in the
country.   They had occupied the country for
some centuries at the time when our story be-
gins—the province being governed by a line of
princes—almost, if not quite, independent sovereigns—called the *Dukes of Normandy*.

The first Duke of Normandy, and the found-
er of the line—the chieftain who originally in-
vaded and conquered the country—was a wild
and half-savage hero from the north, named
Rollo.   He is often, in history, called Rollo the
Dane.   Norway was his native land.   He was
a chieftain by birth there, and, being of a wild
and adventurous disposition, he collected a band
of followers, and committed with them so many
piracies and robberies, that at length the king
of the country expelled him.

Rollo seems not to have considered this ban-
ishment as any very great calamity, since, far

from interrupting his career of piracy and plunder, it only widened the field on which he was to pursue it. He accordingly increased the equipment and the force of his fleet, enlisted more followers, and set sail across the northern part of the German Ocean toward the British shores.

Off the northwestern coast of Scotland there are some groups of mountainous and gloomy islands, which have been, in many different periods of the world, the refuge of fugitives and outlaws. Rollo made these islands his rendezvous now; and he found collected there many other similar spirits, who had fled to these lonely retreats, some on account of political disturbances in which they had become involved, and some on account of their crimes. Rollo's impetuous, ardent, and self-confident character inspired them with new energy and zeal. They gathered around him as their leader. Finding his strength thus increasing, he formed a scheme of concentrating all the force that he could command, so as to organize a grand expedition to proceed to the southward, and endeavor to find some pleasant country which they could seize and settle upon, and make their own. The desperate adventurers around him were

ready enough to enter into this scheme.   The
fleet was refitted, provisioned, and equipped.
The expedition was organized, arms and munitions of war provided, and when all was ready
they set sail.   They had no definite plan in
respect to the place of their destination, their
intention being to make themselves a home on
the first favorable spot that they should find.

They moved southward, cruising at first
along the coast of Scotland, and then of England.   They made several fruitless attempts
to land on the English shores, but were every
where repulsed.   The time when these events
took place was during the reign of Alfred the
Great.   Through Alfred's wise and efficient
measures the whole of his frontier had been
put into a perfect state of defense, and Rollo
found that there was no hope for him there.
He accordingly moved on toward the Straits of
Dover ; but, before passing them, he made a
descent upon the coast of Flanders.   Here there
was a country named Hainault.   It was governed by a potentate called the Count of Hainault.   Rollo made war upon him, defeated him
in battle, took him prisoner, and then compelled
the countess his wife to raise and pay him an
immense sum for his ransom.   Thus he replen-

ished his treasury by an exploit which was considered in those days very great and glorious. To perpetrate such a deed now, unless it were on a *very* great scale, would be to incur the universal reprobation of mankind; but Rollo, by doing it then, not only enriched his coffers, but acquired a very extended and honorable fame.

For some reason or other, Rollo did not attempt to take permanent possession of Hainault, but, after receiving his ransom money, and replenishing his ammunition and stores, he sailed away with his fleet, and, turning westward, he passed through the Straits of Dover, and cruised along the coast of France. He found that the country on the French side of the channel, though equally rich and beautiful with the opposite shore, was in a very different state of defense. He entered the mouth of the Seine. He was embarrassed at first by the difficulties of the navigation in entering the river; but as there was no efficient enemy to oppose him, he soon triumphed over these difficulties, and, once fairly in the river, he found no difficulty in ascending to Rouen.*

In the mean time, the King of France, whose

* See the map at the commencement of this chapter.

name was Charles, and who is generally designated in history as Charles the Simple, began
to collect an army to meet the invader.   Rollo,
however, had made himself master of Rouen
before Charles was able to offer him any effectual opposition.   Rouen was already a strong
place, but Rollo made it stronger.   He enlarged
and repaired the fortifications, built store-houses,
established a garrison, and, in a word, made all
the arrangements requisite for securing an impregnable position for himself and his army.

A long and obstinate war followed between
Rollo and Charles, Rollo being almost uniform-
ly victorious in the combats that took place.
Rollo became more and more proud and imperious in proportion to his success.   He drove the
French king from port to port, and from field
to field, until he made himself master of a large
part of the north of France, over which he
gradually established a regular government of
his own.   Charles struggled in vain to resist
these encroachments.   Rollo continually defeated him ; and finally he shut him up and
besieged him in Paris itself.   At length Charles
was compelled to enter into negotiations for
peace.   Rollo demanded that the large and rich
tract on both sides of the Seine, next the sea—

the same, in fact, that now constitutes Normandy—should be ceded to him and his followers for their permanent possession. Charles was extremely unwilling thus to alienate a part of his kingdom. He would not consent to cede it absolutely and entirely, so as to make it an independent realm. It should be a *dukedom*, and not a separate *kingdom*, so that it might continue still a part of his own royal domains—Rollo to reign over it as a duke, and to acknowledge a general allegiance to the French king. Rollo agreed to this. The war had been now protracted so long that he began himself to desire repose. It was more than thirty years since the time of his landing.

Charles had a daughter named Giselle, and it was a part of the treaty of peace that she should become Rollo's wife. He also agreed to become a Christian. Thus there were, in the execution of the treaty, three ceremonies to be performed. First, Rollo was to *do homage*, as it was called, for his duchy; for it was the custom in those days for subordinate princes, who held their possessions of some higher and more strictly sovereign power, to perform certain ceremonies in the presence of their superior lord, which was called doing homage. These cere-

monies were of various kinds in different countries, though they were all intended to express
the submission of the dependent prince to the
superior authority and power of the higher potentate of whom he held his lands. This act
of homage was therefore to be performed, and
next to the homage was to come the baptism,
and after the baptism, the marriage.

When, however, the time came for the performance of the first of these ceremonies, and all
the great chieftains and potentates of the respective armies were assembled to witness it,
Rollo, it was found, would not submit to what
the customs of the French monarchy required.
He ought to kneel before the king, and put his
hands, clasped together, between the king's
hands, in token of submission, and then to kiss
his foot, which was covered with an elegantly
fashioned slipper on such occasions. Rollo
would do all except the last; but that, no re-
monstrances, urgencies, or persuasions would
induce him to consent to.

And yet it was not a very unusual sign or
token of political subordination to sovereign
power in those days. The pope had exacted it
even of an emperor a hundred years before;
and it is continued by that dignitary to the

present day, on certain state occasions; though
in the case of the pope, there is embroidered
on the slipper which the kneeling suppliant
kisses, a *cross*, so that he who humbles himself
to this ceremony may consider, if he pleases,
that it is that sacred symbol of the divine Re-
deemer's sufferings and death that he so rev-
erently kisses, and not the human foot by which
it is covered.

Rollo could not be made to consent, himself,
to kiss King Charles's foot; and, finally, the
difficulty was compromised by his agreeing to do
it by proxy. He ordered one of his courtiers
to perform that part of the ceremony. The
courtier obeyed, but when he came to lift the
foot, he did it so rudely and lifted it so high as
to turn the monarch over off his seat. This
made a laugh, but Rollo was too powerful for
Charles to think of resenting it.

A few days after this Rollo was baptized
in the cathedral church at Rouen, with great
pomp and parade; and then, on the following
week, he was married to Giselle. The din of
war in which he had lived for more than thirty
years was now changed into festivities and rejoicings. He took full and peaceable possession
of his dukedom, and governed it for the remain-

der of his days with great wisdom, and lived in great prosperity. He made it, in fact, one of the richest and most prosperous realms in Europe, and laid the foundations of still higher degrees of greatness and power, which were gradually developed after his death. And this was the origin of Normandy.

It appears thus that this part of France was seized by Rollo and his Northmen partly because it was nearest at hand to them, being accessible from the English Channel through the River Seine, and partly on account of its exceeding richness and fertility. It has been famous in every age as the garden of France, and travelers at the present day gaze upon its picturesque and beautiful scenery with the highest admiration and pleasure. And yet the scenes which are there presented to the view are wholly unlike those which constitute picturesque and beautiful rural scenery in England and America. In Normandy, the land is not inclosed. No hedges, fences, or walls break the continuity of the surface, but vast tracts spread in every direction, divided into plots and squares, of various sizes and forms, by the varieties of cultivation, like a vast carpet of an irregular tessellated pattern, and varied in the color by a thou-

sand hues of brown and green.　Here and there
vast forests extend, where countless thousands
of trees, though ancient and venerable in form,
stand in rows, mathematically arranged, as they
were planted centuries ago.　These are royal
demesnes, and hunting grounds, and parks connected with the country palaces of the kings or
the chateaux of the ancient nobility.　The cul-
tivators of the soil live, not, as in America, in
little farm-houses built along the road-sides and
dotting the slopes of the hills, but in compact
villages, consisting of ancient dwellings of brick
or stone, densely packed together along a single
street, from which the laborers issue, in picturesque dresses, men and women together, every
morning, to go miles, perhaps, to the scene of
their daily toil.　Except these villages, and the
occasional appearance of an ancient chateau, no
habitations are seen.　The country seems a vast
solitude, teeming every where, however, with
fertility and beauty.　The roads which traverse
these scenes are magnificent avenues, broad,
straight, continuing for many miles an undevi-
ating course over the undulations of the land,
with nothing to separate them from the expanse of cultivation and fruitfulness on either
hand but rows of ancient and venerable trees.

Between these rows of trees the traveler sees
an interminable vista extending both before him
and behind him.   In England, the public road
winds beautifully between walls overhung with
shrubbery, or hedge-rows, with stiles or gateways here and there, revealing hamlets or cot-
tages, which appear and disappear in a rapid
and endlessly varied succession, as the road
meanders, like a rivulet, between its beautiful
banks.   In a word, the public highway in England is beautiful; in France it is grand.

The greatest city in Normandy in modern
times is Rouen, which is situated, as will be
seen by referring to the map at the commencement of this chapter, on the Seine, half way
between Paris and the sea.   At the mouth of
the Seine, or, rather, on the northern shore of
the estuary which forms the mouth of the river,
is a small inlet, which has been found to afford,
on the whole, the best facilities for a harbor
that can be found on the whole line of the
coast.   Even this little port, however, is so
filled up with sand, that when the water re-
cedes at low tide it leaves the shipping all
aground.   The inlet would, in fact, probably
become filled up entirely were it not for artifi-
cial means taken to prevent it.   There are

locks and gateways built in such a manner as to retain a large body of water until the tide is down, and then these gates are opened, and the water is allowed to rush out all together, carrying with it the mud and sand which had begun to accumulate. This haven, being, on the whole, the best and most commodious on the coast, was called *the* harbor, or, as the French expressed it in their language, *le hâvre*, the word *havre* meaning harbor. In fact, the name was in full *le havre de grace*, as if the Normans considered it a matter of special good luck to have even such a chance of a harbor as this at the mouth of their river. The English world have, however, dropped all except the principal word from this long phrase of designation, and call the port simply Havre.

From Rollo the line of Dukes of Normandy continued in uninterrupted succession down to the time of William, a period of about a hundred and fifty years. The country increased all the time in wealth, in population, and in prosperity. The original inhabitants were not, however, expelled; they remained as peasants, herdsmen, and agriculturists, while the Norman chieftains settled over them, holding severally

large estates of land which William granted
them.   The races gradually became intermin-
gled, though they continued for many centuries to evince the superior spirit and energy
which was infused into the population by the
Norman stock.   In fact, it is thought by many
observers that that superiority continues to the
present day.

Chapter II.

Birth of William.

ALTHOUGH Rouen is now very far before all the other cities of Normandy in point of magnitude and importance, and though Rollo, in his conquest of the country, made it his principal head-quarters and his main stronghold, it did not continue exclusively the residence of the dukes of Normandy in after years. The father of William the Conqueror was Robert, who became subsequently the duke, the sixth in the line. He resided, at the time when William was born, in a great castle at Falaise. Falaise, as will be seen upon the map, is west of Rouen, and it stands, like Rouen, at some distance from the sea. The castle was built upon a hill, at a little distance from the town. It has long since ceased to be habitable, but the ruins still remain, giving a picturesque but mournful beauty to the eminence which they crown. They are often visited by travelers, who go to see the place where the great hero and conqueror was born.

The hill on which the old castle stands term-
inates, on one side, at the foot of the castle
walls, in a precipice of rocks, and on two other
sides, also, the ascent is too steep to be practi-
cable for an enemy.   On the fourth side there
is a more gradual declivity, up which the fortress could be approached by means of a winding roadway.   At the foot of this roadway was
the town.   The access to the castle from the
town was defended by a ditch and draw-bridge,
with strong towers on each side of the gate-
way to defend the approach.   There was a
beautiful stream of water which meandered
along through the valley, near the town, and,
after passing it, it disappeared, winding around
the foot of the precipice which the castle crowned.
The castle inclosures were shut in with walls
of stone of enormous thickness; so thick, in
fact, they were, that some of the apartments
were built in the body of the wall.   There were
various buildings within the inclosure.   There
was, in particular, one large, square tower,
several stories in height, built of white stone.
This tower, it is said, still stands in good preservation.   There was a chapel, also, and various other buildings and apartments within the
walls, for the use of the ducal family and their

numerous retinue of servants and attendants, for the storage of munitions of war, and for the garrison.   There were watch-towers on the corners of the walls, and on various lofty projecting pinnacles, where solitary sentinels watched, the livelong day and night, for any approaching danger.   These sentinels looked down on a broad expanse of richly-cultivated country, fields beautified with groves of trees, and with the various colors presented by the changing vegetation, while meandering streams gleamed with their silvery radiance among them, and hamlets of laborers and peasantry were scattered here and there, giving life and animation to the scene.

We have said that William's father was Robert, the sixth Duke of Normandy, so that William himself, being his immediate successor, was the seventh in the line.   And as it is the design of these narratives not merely to amuse the reader with what is entertaining as a tale, but to impart substantial historical knowledge, we must prepare the way for the account of William's birth, by presenting a brief chronological view of the whole ducal line, extending from Rollo to William.   We recommend to the reader to examine with special attention this brief

28—3

account of William's ancestry, for the true
causes which led to William's invasion of England can not be fully appreciated without thoroughly understanding certain important trans-
actions in which some members of the family
of his ancestors were concerned before he was
born. This is particularly the case with the
Lady Emma, who, as will be seen by the following summary, was the sister of the third
duke in the line. The extraordinary and eventful history of her life is so intimately connected
with the subsequent exploits of William, that
it is necessary to relate it in full, and it be-
comes, accordingly, the subject of one of the
subsequent chapters of this volume.

Chronological History of the Norman Line.

Rollo, first Duke of Normandy.
From A.D. 912 to A.D. 917.

It was about 870 that Rollo was banished
from Norway, and a few years after that, at
most, that he landed in France. It was not,
however, until 912 that he concluded his treaty
of peace with Charles, so as to be fully invested
with the title of Duke of Normandy.

He was advanced in age at this time, and,
after spending five years in settling the affairs

of his realm, he resigned his dukedom into the
hands of his son, that he might spend the remainder of his days in rest and peace. He died
in 922, five years after his resignation.

WILLIAM I., second Duke of Normandy.
From 917 to 942.

William was Rollo's son. He began to reign,
of course, five years before his father's death.
He had a quiet and prosperous reign of about
twenty-five years, but he was assassinated at
last by a political enemy, in 942.

RICHARD I., third Duke of Normandy.
From 942 to 996.

He was only ten years old when his father
was assassinated. He became involved in long
and arduous wars with the King of France,
which compelled him to call in the aid of more
Northmen from the Baltic. His new allies, in
the end, gave him as much trouble as the old
enemy, with whom they came to help William
contend ; and he found it very hard to get them
away. He wanted, at length, to make peace
with the French king, and to have them leave
his dominions ; but they said, " That was not
what they came for."

Richard had a beautiful daughter, named
Emma, who afterward became a very import-

ant political personage, as will be seen more
fully in a subsequent chapter.

Richard died in 996, after reigning fifty-four
years.

RICHARD II., fourth Duke of Normandy.
From 996 to 1026.

Richard II. was the son of Richard I., and as
his father had been engaged during his reign in
contentions with his sovereign lord, the King of
France, he, in his turn, was harassed by long-
continued struggles with his vassals, the barons
and nobles of his own realm.   He, too, sent for
Northmen to come and assist him.   During his
reign there was a great contest in England between the Saxons and the Danes, and Ethelred, who was the Saxon claimant to the throne,
came to Normandy, and soon afterward married the Lady Emma, Richard's sister.   The
particulars of this event, from which the most
momentous consequences were afterward seen
to flow, will be given in full in a future chapter.   Richard died in 1026.   He left two sons,
Richard and Robert.   William the Conqueror
was the son of the youngest, and was born two
years before this Richard II. died.

RICHARD III., fifth Duke of Normandy.
From 1026 to 1028.

He was the oldest brother, and, of course, succeeded to the dukedom. His brother Robert was then only a baron—his son William, afterward the Conqueror, being then about two years old. Robert was very ambitious and aspiring, and eager to get possession of the dukedom himself. He adopted every possible means to circumvent and supplant his brother, and, as is supposed, shortened his days by the anxiety and vexation which he caused him; for Richard died suddenly and mysteriously only two years after his accession. It was supposed by some, in fact, that he was poisoned, though there was never any satisfactory proof of this.

Robert, sixth Duke of Normandy.
From 1028 to 1035.

Robert, of course, succeeded his brother, and then, with the characteristic inconsistency of selfishness and ambition, he employed all the power of his realm in helping the King of France to subdue his younger brother, who was evincing the same spirit of seditiousness and insubmission that he had himself displayed. His assistance was of great importance to King Henry; it, in fact, decided the contest in his favor; and thus one younger brother was put down in the commencement of his career of turbulence

and rebellion, by another who had successfully
accomplished a precisely similar course of crime.
King Henry was very grateful for the service
thus rendered, and was ready to do all in his
power, at all times, to co-operate with Robert
in the plans which the latter might form. Robert died in 1035, when William was about
eleven years old.

And here we close this brief summary of the
history of the ducal line, as we have already
passed the period of William's birth; and we
return, accordingly, to give in detail some of
the particulars of that event.

Although the dukes of Normandy were very
powerful potentates, reigning, as they did, almost in the character of independent sovereigns,
over one of the richest and most populous territories of the globe, and though William the
Conqueror was the son of one of them, his birth
was nevertheless very ignoble. His mother
was not the wife of Robert his father, but a
poor peasant girl, the daughter of an humble
tanner of Falaise; and, indeed, William's father, Robert, was not himself the duke at this
time, but a simple baron, as his father was
still living. It was not even certain that he

WILLIAM AND ARLOTTE.

ever would be the duke, as his older brother, who, of course, would come before him, was also then alive. Still, as the son and prospective heir of the reigning duke, his rank was very high.

The circumstances of Robert's first acquaintance with the tanner's daughter were these. He was one day returning home to the castle from some expedition on which he had been sent by his father, when he saw a group of peasant girls standing on the margin of the brook, washing clothes. They were barefooted, and their dress was in other respects disarranged. There was one named Arlotte,* the daughter of a tanner of the town, whose countenance and figure seem to have captivated the young baron. He gazed at her with admiration and pleasure as he rode along. Her complexion was fair, her eyes full and blue, and the expression of her countenance was frank, and open, and happy. She was talking joyously and merrily with her companions as Robert passed, little dreaming of the conspicuous place on the page of English history which she was to occupy, in all future time, in connection with the gay horseman who was riding by.

* Her name is spelled variously, Arlette, Arlotte, Harlotte, and in other ways.

The etiquette of royal and ducal palaces and castles in those days, as now, forbade that a noble of such lofty rank should marry a peasant girl. Robert could not, therefore, have Arlotte for his wife; but there was nothing to prevent his proposing her coming to the castle and living with him—that is, nothing but the law of God, and this was an authority to which dukes and barons in the Middle Ages were accustomed to pay very little regard. There was not even a public sentiment to forbid this, for a nobility like that of England and France in the Middle Ages stands so far above all the mass of society as to be scarcely amenable at all to the ordinary restrictions and obligations of social life. And even to the present day, in those countries where dukes exist, public sentiment seems to tolerate pretty generally whatever dukes see fit to do.

Accordingly, as soon as Robert had arrived at the castle, he sent a messenger from his retinue of attendants down to the village, to the father of Arlotte, proposing that she should come to the castle. The father seems to have had some hesitation in respect to his duty. It is said that he had a brother who was a monk, or rather hermit, who lived a life of reading, med-

itation, and prayer, in a solitary place not far
from Falaise. Arlotte's father sent immediately to this religious recluse for his spiritual
counsel. The monk replied that it was right
to comply with the wishes of so great a man,
whatever they might be. The tanner, thus relieved of all conscientious scruples on the subject by this high religious authority, and rejoicing in the opening tide of prosperity and
distinction which he foresaw for his family
through the baron's love, robed and decorated
his daughter, like a lamb for the sacrifice, and
sent her to the castle.

Arlotte had one of the rooms assigned her,
which was built in the thickness of the wall.
It communicated by a door with the other apartments and inclosures within the area, and there
were narrow windows in the masonry without,
through which she could look out over the broad
expanse of beautiful fields and meadows which
were smiling below. Robert seems to have loved
her with sincere and strong affection, and to
have done all in his power to make her happy.
Her room, however, could not have been very
sumptuously furnished, although she was the
favorite in a ducal castle—at least so far as we
can judge from the few glimpses we get of the

interior through the ancient chroniclers' stories. One story is, that when William was born, his first exploit was to grasp a handful of straw, and to hold it so tenaciously in his little fist that the nurse could scarcely take it away. The nurse was greatly delighted with this infantile prowess; she considered it an omen, and predicted that the babe would some day signalize himself by seizing and holding great possessions. The prediction would have been forgotten if William had not become the conqueror of England at a future day. As it was, it was remembered and recorded; and it suggests to our imagination a very different picture of the conveniences and comforts of Arlotte's chamber from those presented to the eye in ducal palaces now, where carpets of velvet silence the tread on marble floors, and favorites repose under silken canopies on beds of down.

The babe was named William, and he was a great favorite with his father. He was brought up at Falaise. Two years after his birth, Robert's father died, and his oldest brother, Richard III., succeeded to the ducal throne. In two years more, which years were spent in contention between the brothers, Richard also died, and then Robert himself came into possession of the castle in his own name, reigning there over all the cities and domains of Normandy.

William was, of course, now about four years old. He was a bright and beautiful boy, and he grew more and more engaging every year. His father, instead of neglecting and disowning him, as it might have been supposed he would do, took a great deal of pride and pleasure in witnessing the gradual development of his powers and his increasing attractiveness, and he openly acknowledged him as his son.

In fact, William was a universal favorite about the castle. When he was five and six years old he was very fond of playing the soldier. He would marshal the other boys of the castle, his playmates, into a little troop, and train them around the castle inclosures, just as ardent and aspiring boys do with their comrades now. He possessed a certain vivacity and spirit too, which gave him, even then, a great ascendency over his playfellows. He invented their plays; he led them in their mischief; he settled their disputes. In a word, he possessed a temperament and character which enabled him very easily and strongly to hold the position which his rank as son of the lord of the castle so naturally assigned him.

A few years thus passed away, when, at length, Robert conceived the design of making a pilgrimage to the Holy Land. This was a plan, not of humble-minded piety, but of ambition for fame. To make a pilgrimage to the Holy Land was a romantic achievement that covered whoever accomplished it with a sort of sombre glory, which, in the case of a prince or potentate, mingled with, and hallowed and exalted, his military renown. Robert determined on making the pilgrimage. It was a distant and dangerous journey. In fact, the difficulties and dangers of the way were perhaps what chiefly imparted to the enterprise its romance, and gave it its charms. It was customary for kings and rulers, before setting out, to arrange all the affairs of their kingdoms, to provide a regency to govern during their absence, and to determine upon their successors, so as to provide for the very probable contingency of their not living to return.

As soon, therefore, as Robert announced his plan of a pilgrimage, men's minds were immediately turned to the question of the succession. Robert had never been married, and he had consequently no son who was entitled to succeed him. He had two brothers, and also a cousin, and some other relatives, who had claims to the succession. These all began to maneuver among the chieftains and nobles, each endeavoring to prepare the way for having his own claims advanced, while Robert himself was secretly determining that the little William should be his heir. He said nothing about this, however, but he took care to magnify the importance of his little son in every way, and to bring him as much as possible into public notice. William, on his part, possessed so much personal beauty, and so many juvenile accomplishments, that he became a great favorite with all the nobles, and chieftains, and knights who saw him, sometimes at his father's castle, and sometimes away from home, in their own fortresses or towns, where his father took him, from time to time, in his train.

At length, when affairs were ripe for their consummation, Duke Robert called together a grand council of all the subordinate dukes, and earls, and barons of his realm, to make known to them the plan of his pilgrimage. They came together from all parts of Normandy, each in a splendid cavalcade, and attended by an armed retinue of retainers. When the assembly had been convened, and the preliminary forms and

ceremonies had been disposed of, Robert announced his grand design.

As soon as he had concluded, one of the nobles, whose name and title was Guy, count of
Burgundy, rose and addressed the duke in reply. He was sorry, he said, to hear that the
duke, his cousin, entertained such a plan. He
feared for the safety of the realm when the
chief ruler should be gone. All the estates of
the realm, he said, the barons, the knights, the
chieftains and soldiers of every degree, would
be all without a head.

"Not so," said Robert: "I will leave you a
master in my place." Then, pointing to the
beautiful boy by his side, he added, "I have a
little fellow here, who, though he is little now,
I acknowledge, will grow bigger by and by,
with God's grace, and I have great hopes that
he will become a brave and gallant man. I
present him to you, and from this time forth I
give him *seizin** of the Duchy of Normandy
as my known and acknowledged heir. And I
appoint Alan, duke of Brittany, governor of
Normandy in my name until I shall return,
and in case I shall not return, in the name of

---

* *Seizin*, an ancient feudal term denoting the inducting of
a party to a legal possession of his right.

William my son, until he shall become of manly age."

The assembly was taken wholly by surprise at this announcement. Alan, duke of Brittany, who was one of the chief claimants to the succession, was pleased with the honor conferred upon him in making him at once the governor of the realm, and was inclined to prefer the present certainty of governing at once in the name of others, to the remote contingency of reigning in his own. The other claimants to the inheritance were confounded by the suddenness of the emergency, and knew not what to say or do. The rest of the assembly were pleased with the romance of having the beautiful boy for their feudal sovereign. The duke saw at once that every thing was favorable to the accomplishment of his design. He took the lad in his arms, kissed him, and held him out in view of the assembly. William gazed around upon the panoplied warriors before him with a bright and beaming eye. They knelt down as by a common accord to do him homage, and then took the oath of perpetual allegiance and fidelity to his cause.

Robert thought, however, that it would not be quite prudent to leave his son himself in the

28—4

custody of these his rivals, so he took him with him to Paris when he set out upon his pilgrimage, with a view of establishing him there, in the court of Henry, the French king, while he should himself be gone. Young William was presented to the French king, on a day set apart for the ceremony, with great pomp and parade. The king held a special court to receive him. He seated himself on his throne in a grand apartment of his palace, and was surrounded by his nobles and officers of state, all magnificently dressed for the occasion. At the proper time, Duke Robert came in, dressed in his pilgrim's garb, and leading young William by the hand. His attendant pilgrim knights accompanied him. Robert led the boy to the feet of their common sovereign, and, kneeling there, ordered William to kneel too, to do homage to the king. King Henry received him very graciously. He embraced him, and promised to receive him into his court, and to take the best possible care of him while his father was away. The courtiers were very much struck with the beauty and noble bearing of the boy. His countenance beamed with an animated, but yet very serious expression, as he was somewhat awed by the splendor of the scene around him. He was himself then nine years old.

CHAPTER III.

THE ACCESSION.

AFTER spending a little time at Paris, Robert took leave of the king, and of William his son, and went forth, with a train of attendant knights, on his pilgrimage. He had a great variety of adventures, which can not be related here, as it is the history of the son, and not of the father, which is the subject of this narrative. Though he traveled strictly as a pilgrim, it was still with great pomp and parade. After visiting Rome, and accomplishing various services and duties connected with his pilgrimage there, he laid aside his pilgrim's garb, and, assuming his proper rank as a great Norman chieftain, he went to Constantinople, where he made a great display of his wealth and magnificence. At the time of the grand procession, for example, by which he entered the city of Constantinople, he rode a mule, which, besides being gorgeously caparisoned, had shoes of gold instead of iron; and these shoes were purposely attached so slightly to the hoofs, that they were shaken off as the animal walked along, to be picked up by the populace. This was to impress them with grand ideas of the rider's wealth and splendor. After leaving Constantinople, Robert resumed his pilgrim's garb, and went on toward the Holy Land.

The journey, however, did not pass without the usual vicissitudes of so long an absence and so distant a pilgrimage. At one time Robert was sick, and, after lingering for some time in a fever, he so far recovered his strength as to be borne on a litter by the strength of other men, though he could not advance himself, either on horseback or on foot; and as for traveling carriages, there had been no such invention in those days. They made arrangements, therefore, for carrying the duke on a litter. There were sixteen Moorish slaves employed to serve as his bearers. This company was divided into sets, four in each, the several sets taking the burden in rotation. Robert and his attendant knights looked down with great contempt on these black pagan slaves. One day the cavalcade was met by a Norman who was returning home to Normandy after having accomplished his pilgrimage. He asked Duke Robert if he had any message to send to his friends at home.

" Yes," said he ; " tell them you saw me here, on my way to Paradise, carried by sixteen *de-mons.*"

Robert reached Jerusalem, and set out on his return ; and soon after rumors came back to Paris that he had died on his way home. The accounts of the manner of his death were contradictory and uncertain ; but the fact was soon made sure, and the news produced every where a great sensation.   It soon appeared that the brothers and cousins of Robert, who had claimed the right to succeed him in preference to his son William, had only suspended their claims—they had not abandoned them.   They began to gather their forces, each in his own separate domain, and to prepare to take the field, if necessary, in vindication of what they considered their rights to the inheritance.   In a word, their oaths of fealty to William were all forgotten, and each claimant was intent only on getting possession himself of the ducal crown.

In the mean time, William himself was at Paris, and only eleven years of age.   He had been receiving a careful education there, and was a very prepossessing and accomplished young prince.   Still, he was yet but a mere boy.   He had been under the care of a milita-

ry tutor, whose name was Theroulde. Theroulde was a veteran soldier, who had long been
in the employ of the King of France. He took
great interest in his young pupil's progress.
He taught him to ride and to practice all the
evolutions of horsemanship which were required
by the tactics of those days. He trained him,
too, in the use of arms, the bow and arrow, the
javelin, the sword, the spear, and accustomed
him to wear, and to exercise in, the armor of
steel with which warriors were used, in those
days, to load themselves in going into battle.
Young princes like William had suits of this
armor made for them, of small size, which they
were accustomed to wear in private in their
military exercises and trainings, and to appear
in, publicly, on great occasions of state. These
dresses of iron were of course very heavy and
uncomfortable, but the young princes and dukes
were, nevertheless, very proud and happy to
wear them.

While William was thus engaged in pursu-
ing his military education in Paris, several com-
petitors for his dukedom immediately appeared
in Normandy and took the field. The strongest
and most prominent among them was the Earl
of Arques. His name was William too, but, to

distinguish him from the young duke, we shall call him Arques.   He was a brother of Robert, and maintained that, as Robert left no lawful heir, he was indisputably entitled to succeed him.   Arques assembled his forces and prepared to take possession of the country.

It will be recollected that Robert, when he left Normandy in setting out on his pilgrimage, had appointed a nobleman named Alan to act as regent, or governor of the country, until he should return; or, in case he should never return, until William should become of age.   Alan had a council of officers, called the council of regency, with whose aid he managed the administration of the government.   This council, with Alan at their head, proclaimed young William duke, and immediately began to act in his name.   When they found that the Earl of Arques was preparing to seize the government, they began to assemble their forces also, and thus both sides prepared for war.

Before they actually commenced hostilities, however, the pilgrim knights who had accompanied Robert on his pilgrimage, and who had been journeying home slowly by themselves ever since their leader's death, arrived in Normandy.   These were chieftains and nobles of high rank and influence, and each of the contending parties were eager to have them join their side.   Besides the actual addition of force which these men could bring to the cause they should espouse, the moral support they would give to it was a very important consideration. Their having been on this long and dangerous pilgrimage invested them with a sort of romantic and religious interest in the minds of all the people, who looked up to them, in consequence of it, with a sort of veneration and awe ; and then, as they had been selected by Robert to accompany him on his pilgrimage, and had gone on the long and dangerous journey with him, continuing to attend upon him until he died, they were naturally regarded as his most faithful and confidential friends.   For these and similar reasons, it was obvious that the cause which they should espouse in the approaching contest would gain a large accession of moral power by their adhesion.

As soon as they arrived in Normandy, rejecting all proposals from other quarters, they joined young William's cause with the utmost promptitude and decision.   Alan received them at once into his councils.   An assembly was convened, and the question was discussed whether William should be sent for to come to Normandy. Some argued that he was yet a mere boy, incapable of rendering them any real service in the impending contest, while he would be exposed, more perhaps than they themselves, to be taken captive or slain. They thought it best, therefore, that he should remain, for the present, in Paris, under the protection of the French king.

Others, on the other hand, contended that the influence of William's presence, boy as he was, would animate and inspire all his followers, and awaken every where, throughout the country, a warm interest in his cause; that his very tenderness and helplessness would appeal strongly to every generous heart, and that his youthful accomplishments and personal charms would enlist thousands in his favor, who would forget, and perhaps abandon him, if he kept away. Besides, it was by no means certain that he was so safe as some might suppose in King Henry's custody and power. King Henry might himself lay claims to the vacant duchy, with a view of bestowing it upon some favorite of his own, in which case he might confine young William in one of his castles, in an honorable, but still rigid and hopeless captivity, or treacherously destroy his life by the secret administration of poison.

These latter counsels prevailed. Alan and the nobles who were with him sent an embassage to the court of King Henry to bring William home. Henry made objections and difficulties. This alarmed the nobles. They feared that it would prove true that Henry himself had designs on Normandy. They sent a new embassage, with demands more urgent than before. Finally, after some time spent in negotiations and delays, King Henry concluded to yield, and William set out on his return. He was now about twelve or thirteen years old. His military tutor, Theroulde, accompanied him, and he was attended likewise by the embassadors whom Alan had sent for him, and by a strong escort for his protection by the way. He arrived in safety at Alan's head-quarters.

William's presence in Normandy had the effect which had been anticipated from it. It awakened every where a great deal of enthusiasm in his favor. The soldiers were pleased to see how handsome their young commander was in form, and how finely he could ride. He was, in fact, a very superior equestrian for one so young. He was more fond, even, than other boys of horses; and as, of course, the most graceful and the fleetest horses which could be found were provided for him, and as Theroulde had given him the best and most complete instruction, he made a fine display as he rode swiftly through the camp, followed by veteran nobles, splendidly dressed and mounted, and happy to be in his train, while his own countenance beamed with a radiance in which native intelligence and beauty were heightened by the animation and excitement of pride and pleasure. In respect to the command of the army, of course the real power remained in Alan's hands, but every thing was done in William's name; and in respect to all external marks and symbols of sovereignty, the beautiful boy seemed to possess the supreme command; and as the sentiment of loyalty is always the strongest when the object which calls for the exercise of it is most helpless or frail, Alan found his power very much increased when he had this beautiful boy to exhibit as the true and rightful heir, in whose name and for whose benefit all his power was held.

Still, however, the country was very far from becoming settled. The Earl of Arques kept the field, and other claimants, too, strengthened themselves in their various castles and towns, as if preparing to resist. In those days, every separate district of the country was almost a separate realm, governed by its own baron, who lived, with his retainers, within his own castle walls, and ruled the land around him with a rod of iron. These barons were engaged in perpetual quarrels among themselves, each plundering the dominions of the rest, or making hostile incursions into the territories of a neighbor to revenge some real or imaginary wrong. This turbulence and disorder prevailed every where throughout Normandy at the time of William's return. In the general confusion, William's government scarcely knew who were his friends or his enemies. At one time, when a deputation was sent to some of the barons in William's name, summoning them to come with their forces and join his standard, as they were in duty bound to do, they felt independent enough to send back word to him that they had "too much to do in settling their own quarrels to be able to pay any attention to his."

In the course of a year or two, moreover, and while his own realm continued in this unsettled and distracted state, William became involved in what was almost a quarrel with King Henry himself.   When he was fifteen years old, which was two or three years after his return from Paris to Normandy, Henry sent directions to William to come to a certain town, called Evreux, situated about half way between Falaise and Paris, and just within the confines of Normandy,* to do homage to him there for his duchy.   There was some doubt among William's counselors whether it would be most prudent to obey or disobey this command.   They finally concluded that it was best to obey. Grand preparations were accordingly made for the expedition; and, when all was ready, the young duke was conducted in great state, and with much pomp and parade, to meet his sovereign.

The interview between William and his sovereign, and the ceremonies connected with it, lasted some days.   In the course of this time, William remained at Evreux, and was, in some sense, of course, in Henry's power.   William, having been so long in Henry's court as a mere boy, accustomed all the time to look up to and obey Henry as a father, regarded him somewhat in that light now, and approached him with great deference and respect.   Henry re-

* See map at the commencement of chapter ix.

ceived him in a somewhat haughty and imperious manner, as if he considered him still under the same subjection as heretofore.

William had a fortress or castle on the frontiers of his dukedom, toward Henry's dominions.   The name of the castle was Tellières,
and the governor of it was a faithful old soldier
named De Crespin.   William's father, Robert,
had intrusted De Crespin with the command of
the castle, and given him a garrison to defend
it.   Henry now began to make complaint to
William in respect to this castle.   The garrison, he said, were continually making incursions into his dominions.   William replied that
he was very sorry that there was cause for such
a complaint.   He would inquire into it, and if
the fact were really so, he would have the evil
immediately corrected.   Henry replied that that
was not sufficient.   " You must deliver up the
castle to me," he said, " to be destroyed."   William was indignant at such a demand; but he
was so accustomed to obey implicitly whatever
King Henry might require of him, that he sent
the order to have the castle surrendered.

When, however, the order came to De Crespin, the governor of the castle, he refused to
obey it.   The fortress, he said, had been com-

mitted to his charge by Robert, duke of Normandy, and he should not give it up to the possession of any foreign power. When this answer was reported to William and his counselors, it made them still more indignant than before at the domineering tyranny of the command, and more disposed than ever to refuse
obedience to it. Still William was in a great
measure in the monarch's power. On cool reflection, they perceived that resistance would
then be vain. New and more authoritative orders were accordingly issued for the surrender
of the castle. De Crespin now obeyed. He
gave up the keys and withdrew with his garrison. William was then allowed to leave Evreux
and return home, and soon afterward the castle
was razed to the ground.

This affair produced, of course, a great deal
of animosity and irritation between the governments of France and Normandy ; and where
such a state of feeling exists between two powers separated only by an imaginary line running through a populous and fertile country,
aggressions from one side and from the other
are sure to follow. These are soon succeeded
by acts of retaliation and revenge, leading, in
the end, to an open and general war. It was

so now. Henry marched his armies into Normandy, seized towns, destroyed castles, and, where he was resisted by the people, he laid waste the country with fire and sword. He finally laid siege to the very castle of Falaise.

William and his government were for a time nearly overwhelmed with the tide of disaster and calamity. The tide turned, however, at length, and the fortune of war inclined in their favor. William rescued the town and castle of Falaise; it was in a very remarkable manner, too, that this exploit was accomplished. The fortress was closely invested with Henry's forces, and was on the very eve of being surrendered. The story is, that Henry had offered bribes to the governor of the castle to give it up to him, and that the governor had agreed to receive them and to betray his trust. While he was preparing to do so, William arrived at the head of a resolute and determined band of Normans. They came with so sudden an onset upon the army of besiegers as to break up their camp and force them to abandon the siege. The people of the town and the garrison of the castle were extremely rejoiced to be thus rescued, and when they came to learn through whose instrumentality they had been saved, and

saw the beautiful horseman whom they remembered as a gay and happy child playing about
the precincts of the castle, they were perfectly
intoxicated with delight.   They filled the air
with the wildest acclamations, and welcomed
William back to the home of his childhood with
manifestations of the most extravagant joy. As
to the traitorous governor, he was dealt with
very leniently.   Perhaps the general feeling of
joy awakened emotions of leniency and forgiveness in William's mind—or perhaps the proof
against the betrayer was incomplete. They
did not, therefore, take his life, which would
have been justly forfeited, according to the military ideas of the times, if he had been really
guilty. They deprived him of his command,
confiscated his property, and let him go free.

After this, William's forces continued for
some time to make head successfully against
those of the King of France; but then, on the
other hand, the danger from his uncle, the Earl
of Arques, increased. The earl took advantage
of the difficulty and danger in which William
was involved in his contests with King Henry,
and began to organize his forces again. He
fortified himself in his castle at Arques,* and

* See map, chapter ix.

28—5

was collecting a large force there.   Arques was
in the northeastern part of Normandy, near the
sea, where the ruins of the ancient castle still
remain.   The earl built an almost impregnable
tower for himself on the summit of the rock
on which the castle stood, in a situation so inaccessible that he thought he could retreat to
it in any emergency, with a few chosen followers, and bid defiance to any assault.   In and
around this castle the earl had got quite a large
army together.   William advanced with his
forces, and, encamping around them, shut them
in.   King Henry, who was then in a distant
part of Normandy, began to put his army in
motion to come to the rescue of Arques.

Things being in this state, William left a
strong body of men to continue the investment
and siege of Arques, and went off himself, at
the head of the remainder of his force, to intercept Henry on his advance.   The result was a
battle and a victory, gained under circumstances so extraordinary, that William, young
as he was, acquired by his exploits a brilliant
and universal renown.

It seems that Henry, in his progress to
Arques, had to pass through a long and gloomy
valley, which was bounded on either side by

precipitous and forest-covered hills. Through
this dangerous defile the long train of Henry's
army was advancing, arranged and marshaled
in such an order as seemed to afford the greatest hope of security in case of an attack. First
came the vanguard, a strong escort, formed of
heavy bodies of soldiery, armed with battle-
axes and pikes, and other similar weapons, the
most efficient then known. Immediately after
this vanguard came a long train of baggage,
the tents, the provisions, the stores, and all the
munitions of war. The baggage was followed
by a great company of servants—the cooks, the
carters, the laborers, the camp followers of every
description—a throng of non-combatants, useless, of course, in a battle, and a burden on a
march, and yet the inseparable and indispensa-
ble attendant of an army, whether at rest or in
motion. After this throng came the main body
of the army, with the king, escorted by his
guard of honor, at the head of it. An active
and efficient corps of lancers and men-at-arms
brought up the rear.

William conceived the design of drawing this
cumbrous and unmanageable body into an ambuscade. He selected, accordingly, the narrow-
est and most dangerous part of the defile for the

purpose, and stationed vast numbers of Norman
soldiers, armed with javelins and arrows, upon
the slopes of the hill on either side, concealing
them all carefully among the thickets and rocks.
He then marshaled the remainder of his forces
in the valley, and sent them up the valley to
meet Henry as he was descending. This body
of troops, which was to advance openly to meet
the king, as if they constituted the whole of
William's force, were to fight a pretended battle with the vanguard, and then to retreat, in
hopes to draw the whole train after them in a
pursuit so eager as to throw them into confusion ; and then, when the column, thus disarranged, should reach the place of ambuscade,
the Normans were to come down upon them
suddenly from their hiding-places, and complete
their discomfiture.

The plan was well laid, and wisely and
bravely executed ; and it was most triumphantly successful in its result. The vanguard of
Henry's army were deceived by the pretended
flight of the Norman detachment. They supposed, too, that it constituted the whole body
of their enemies. They pressed forward, therefore, with great exultation and eagerness to
pursue them. News of the attack, and of the

apparent repulse with which the French soldiers had met it, passed rapidly along the valley,
producing every where the wildest excitement,
and an eager desire to press forward to the
scene of conflict. The whole valley was filled
with shouts and outcries; baggage was abandoned, that those who had charge of it might
hurry on; men ran to and fro for tidings, or
ascended eminences to try to see. Horsemen
drove at full speed from front to rear, and from
rear on to the front again; orders and counter
orders were given, which nobody would understand or attend to in the general confusion and
din. In fact, the universal attention seemed
absorbed in one general and eager desire to
press forward with headlong impetuosity to the
scene of victory and pursuit which they supposed was enacting in the van.

The army pressed on in this confused and
excited manner until they reached the place of
ambuscade. They went on, too, through this
narrow passage, as heedlessly as ever; and,
when the densest and most powerful portion of
the column was crowding through, they were
suddenly thunderstruck by the issuing of a
thousand weapons from the heights and thickets above them on either hand—a dreadful

shower of arrows, javelins, and spears, which struck down hundreds in a moment, and overwhelmed the rest with astonishment and terror. As soon as this first discharge had been effected, the concealed enemy came pouring down the sides of the mountain, springing out from a thousand hiding-places, as if suddenly brought into being by some magic power. The discomfiture of Henry's forces was complete and irremediable. The men fled every where in utter dismay, trampling upon and destroying one another, as they crowded back in terrified throngs to find some place of safety up the valley. There, after a day or two, Henry got together the scattered remains of his army, and established something like a camp.

It is a curious illustration of the feudal feelings of those times in respect to the gradation of ranks, or else of the extraordinary modesty and good sense of William's character, that he assumed no airs of superiority over his sovereign, and showed no signs of extravagant elation after this battle. He sent a respectful embassage to Henry, recognizing his own acknowledged subjection to Henry as his sovereign, and imploring his protection! He looked confidently to him, he said, for aid and support against his rebellious subjects.

Though he thus professed, however, to rely on Henry, he really trusted most, it seems, to his own right arm; for, as soon as this battle was fairly over, and while the whole country was excited with the astonishing brilliancy of the exploit performed by so young a man, William mounted his horse, and calling upon those to follow him who wished to do so, he rode at full speed, at the head of a small cavalcade, to the castle at Arques. His sudden appearance here, with the news of the victory, inspirited the besiegers to such a degree that the castle was soon taken. He allowed the rebel earl to escape, and thus, perhaps, all the more effectually put an end to the rebellion. He was now in peaceable possession of his realm.

He went in triumph to Falaise, where he was solemnly crowned with great ceremony and parade, and all Normandy was filled with congratulations and rejoicings.

72   WILLIAM THE CONQUEROR.

A lapse of twenty years.   Conspiracy of Guy of Burgundy.

CHAPTER IV.

WILLIAM'S REIGN IN NORMANDY.

FROM the time of William's obtaining quiet possession of his realm to his invasion of England, a long period intervened. There was a lapse of more than twenty years. During this long interval, William governed his duchy, suppressed insurrections, built castles and towns, carried on wars, regulated civil institutions, and, in fact, exercised, in a very energetic and successful manner, all the functions of government —his life being diversified all the time by the usual incidents which mark the career of a great military ruler of an independent realm in the Middle Ages. We will give in this chapter a description of some of these incidents.

On one occasion a conspiracy was formed to take his life by secret assassination. A great chieftain, named Guy of Burgundy, William's uncle, was the leader of it, and a half-witted man, named Galet, who occupied the place of jester or fool in William's court, was the means of discovering and exposing it. These *jesters*, of whom there was always one or more in the retinue of every great prince in those days, were either very eccentric or very foolish, or half-insane men, who were dressed fantastically, in gaudy colors and with cap and bells, and were kept to make amusement for the court. The name of William's jester was Galet.

Guy of Burgundy and his fellow-conspirators occupied certain gloomy castles, built in remote and lonely situations on the confines of Normandy. Here they were accustomed to assemble for the purpose of concocting their plans, and gathering their men and their resources— doing every thing in the most cunning and secret manner. Before their scheme was fully ripe for execution, it happened that William made a hunting excursion into the neighborhood of their territory with a small band of followers —such as would be naturally got together on such a party of pleasure. Galet, the fool, was among them.

As soon as Guy and his fellow-conspirators learned that William was so near, they determined to precipitate the execution of their plan, and waylay and assassinate him on his return.

They accordingly left their secret and lonely rendezvous among the mountains one by one,

in order to avoid attracting observation, and
went to a town called Bayeux, through which
they supposed that William would have to pass
on his return. Here they held secret consulta-
tions, and formed their final plans. They sent
out a part of their number, in small bands, into
the region of country which William would
have to cross, to occupy the various roads and
passes, and thus to cut off all possibility of his
escape. They made all these arrangements in
the most secret and cautious manner, and began to think that they were sure of their prey.

It happened, however, that some of William's
attendants, with Galet the fool among them,
had preceded William on his return, and had
reached Bayeux* at the time when the conspirators arrived there. The townspeople did
not observe the coming of the conspirators particularly, as many horsemen and soldiers were
coming and going at that time, and they had
no means of distinguishing the duke's friends
from his enemies; but Galet, as he sauntered
about the town, noticed that there were many
soldiers and knights to be seen who were not
of his master's party. This attracted his attention; he began to watch the motions of these

* See map, chapter ix.

strangers, and to listen, without seeming to
listen, in order to catch the words they spoke
to each other as they talked in groups or passed
one another in the streets.   He was soon satisfied that some mischief was intended.   He immediately threw aside his cap and bells, and his
fantastic dress, and, taking a staff in his hand,
he set off on foot to go back as fast as possible
in search of the duke, and give him the alarm.
He found the duke at a village called Valonges.
He arrived there at night.   He pressed forward
hastily into his master's chamber, half forcing
his way through the attendants, who, accustomed to the liberties which such a personage
as he was accustomed to take on all occasions,
made only a feeble resistance to his wishes.
He found the duke asleep, and he called upon
him with a very earnest voice to awake and
arise immediately, for his life was in danger.

William was at first inclined to disbelieve
the story which Galet told him, and to think
that there was no cause to fear.   He was,
however, soon convinced that Galet was right,
and that there was reason for alarm.   He arose
and dressed himself hastily; and, inasmuch as
a monarch, in the first moments of the discovery of a treasonable plot, knows not whom to

trust, William wisely concluded not to trust
any body. He went himself to the stables,
saddled his horse with his own hand, mounted
him, and rode away. He had a very narrow
escape; for, at the same time, while Galet was
hastening to Valonges to give his master warning of his danger, the conspirators had been advancing to the same place, and had completely
surrounded it; and they were on the eve of
making an attack upon William's quarters at
the very hour when he set out upon his flight.
William had accordingly proceeded only a little way on his route before he heard the footsteps of galloping horses, and the clanking of
arms, on the road behind him. It was a troop
of the conspirators coming, who, finding that
William had fled, had set off immediately in
pursuit. William rode hastily into a wood,
and let them go by.

He remained for some time in his hiding-
place, and then cautiously emerged from it to
continue his way. He did not dare to keep
the public road, although it was night, but took
a wild and circuitous route, in lanes and by-
paths, which conducted him, at length, to the
vicinity of the sea. Here, about day-break, he
was passing a mansion, supposing that no one

WILLIAM'S ESCAPE.

would observe him at so early an hour, when, suddenly, he perceived a man sitting at the gate, armed and equipped, and in an attitude of waiting. He was waiting for his horse. He was a nobleman named Hubert. He recognized William immediately as the duke, and accosted him in a tone of astonishment, saying, " Why, my lord duke, is it possible that this is you ?" He was amazed to see the ruler of the realm out at such an hour, in such a condition, alone, exhausted, his dress all in disorder from the haste with which he had put it on, and his steed breathless and covered with dust, and ready, apparently, to drop down with fatigue and exhaustion.

William, finding that he was recognized, related his story. It appeared, in the end, that Hubert held his own castle and village as a tenant of one of the principal conspirators, and was bound, according to the feudal ideas of the time, to espouse his landlord's cause. He told William, however, that he had nothing to fear. " I will defend your life," said he, " as if it were my own." So saying, he called his three sons, who were all athletic and courageous young men, and commanded them to mount their horses and get ready for a march. He took Will-

iam into his castle, and gave him the food and
refreshment that he needed.   Then he brought
him again into the court-yard of the house,
where William found the three young horsemen
mounted and ready, and a strong and fleet steed
prepared for himself.   He mounted.   Hubert
commanded his sons to conduct the prince with
all dispatch to Falaise, without traveling at all
upon the highway or entering a town.   They
took, accordingly, a straight course across the
country—which was probably then, as now,
nearly destitute of inclosures—and conducted
William safely to his castle at Falaise.

In the course of the morning, William's pursuers came to Hubert's castle, and asked if the
duke had been seen going by.   Hubert replied
in the affirmative, and he mounted his steed
with great readiness to go and show them the
road which the fugitive had taken.   He urged
them to ride hard, in hopes of soon overtaking
the object of their pursuit.   They drove on, accordingly, with great impetuosity and ardor,
under Hubert's guidance; but, as he had purposely taken a wrong road, he was only leading
them further and further astray.   Finally they
gave up the chase, and Hubert returned with
the disappointed pursuers to his fortress, Will-

iam having in the mean time arrived safely at
Falaise.

The conspirators now found that it was useless any longer to attempt to conceal their plans.
In fact, they were already all exposed, and they
knew that William would immediately summon
his troops and come out to seize them. They
must, therefore, either fly from the country or
attempt an open rebellion. They decided on the
latter—the result was a civil war. In the end,
William was victorious. He took a large number of the rebels prisoners, and he adopted the
following very singular plan for inflicting a
suitable punishment upon them, and at the
same time erecting a permanent monument of
his victory. He laid out a public road across
the country, on the line over which he had been
conducted by the sons of Hubert, and compelled
the rebels to make it. A great part of this
country was low and marshy, and had been for
this reason avoided by the public road, which
took a circuitous course around it. The rebel
prisoners were now, however, set at work to
raise a terrace or embankment, on a line sur-
veyed by William's engineers, which followed
almost exactly the course of his retreat. The
high road was then laid out upon this terrace,
    28—6

and it became immediately a public thorough-
fare of great importance. It continued for several centuries one of the most frequented high-
ways in the realm, and was known by the name
of the Raised Road—*Terre levée*—throughout
the kingdom. In fact, the remains of it, ap-
pearing like the ruins of an ancient rail-road
embankment, exist to the present day.

In the course of the war with these rebels a
curious incident occurred at one of the battles,
or, rather, is said to have occurred, by the historians who tell the story, which, if true, illus-
trates very strikingly the romantic and chival-
rous ideas of the times. Just as the battle was
commencing, William perceived a strong and
finely-equipped body of horsemen preparing to
charge upon the very spot where he himself,
surrounded by his officers, was standing. Now
the armor worn by knights in battle in those
times covered and concealed the figure and the
face so fully, that it would have been impossible even for acquaintances and friends to recog-
nize each other, were it not that the knights
were all accustomed to wear certain devices
upon some part of their armor—painted, for instance, upon their shields, or embroidered on
little banners which they bore—by means of

which they might be known. These devices
became at length hereditary in the great families——sons being proud to wear, themselves, the
emblems to which the deeds of their fathers had
imparted a trace of glory and renown. The devices of different chieftains were combined,
sometimes, in cases of intermarriage, or were
modified in various ways; and with these minor
changes they would descend from generation to
generation as the family coat of arms. And
this was the origin of heraldry.

Now the body of horsemen that were advancing to the charge, as above described, had each
of them his device upon a little flag or banner
attached to their lances. As they were advancing, William scrutinized them closely, and presently recognized in their leader a man who had
formerly been upon his side. His name was
Rollo de Tesson. He was one of those who had
sworn fealty to him at the time when his father
Robert presented him to the council, when setting out upon his pilgrimage. William accordingly exclaimed, with a loud voice, " Why, these
are my friends !" The officers and the soldiers
of the body-guard who were with him, taking
up the cry, shouted " *Friends ! friends !*" Rollo de Tesson and the other knights, who were

slowly coming up, preparing to charge upon
William's party, surprised at being thus accosted, paused in their advance, and finally halted.
Rollo said to the other knights, who gathered
around him, " I *was* his friend. I gave my oath
to his father that I would stand by him and defend him with my life; and now I have this
morning sworn to the Count of Cotentin"——the
Count of Cotentin was the leader of the rebellion——" that I would seek out William on the
battle-field, and be the first to give him a blow.
I know not what to do."   " Keep both oaths,"
replied one of his companions.   " Go and strike
him a gentle blow, and then defend him with
your life."   The whole troop seconded this proposal by acclamation. Rollo advanced, followed
by the other knights, with gestures and shouts
denoting that they were friends.   He rode up
to William, told him that he had that morning
sworn to strike him, and then dealt him a pretended blow upon his shoulder ; but as both the
shoulder and the hand which struck it were
armed with steel, the clanking sound was all
the effect that was produced.   Rollo and his
troop——their sworn obligation to the Count of
Cotentin being thus fulfilled——turned now into
the ranks of William's soldiery, and fought val-
iantly all day upon his side.

Although William was generally victorious in the battles that he fought, and succeeded in putting down one rebellion after another with promptness and decision, still, new rebellions and new wars were constantly breaking out, which kept his dominions in a continual state of commotion. In fact, the chieftains, the nobles, and the knights, constituting the only classes of society that exercised any influence, or were regarded with any respect in those days, were never contented except when actively employed in military campaigns. The excitements and the glory of war were the only excitements and glory that they understood, or had the means of enjoying. Their dwellings were great fortresses, built on the summits of the rocks, which, however picturesque and beautiful they appear as *ruins* now, were very gloomy and desolate as residences then. They were attractive enough when their inmates were flying to them for refuge from an enemy, or were employed within the walls in concentrating their forces and brightening up their arms for some new expedition for vengeance or plunder, but they were lonely and lifeless scenes of restlessness and discontent in times of quietness and peace.

It is difficult for us, at this day, to conceive
how destitute of all the ordinary means of comfort and enjoyment, in comparison with a modern dwelling, the ancient feudal castles must
have been.   They were placed in situations as
nearly inaccessible as possible, and the natural
impediments of approach were increased by
walls, and gates, and ditches, and draw-bridges.
The door of access was often a window in the
wall, ten or fifteen feet from the ground, to
which the inmates or their friends mounted by
a ladder.   The floors were of stone, the walls
were naked, the ceiling was a rudely-construct-
ed series of arches.   The apartments, too, were
ordinarily small, and were arranged one above
another, in the successive stories of a tower.
Nor could these cell-like chambers be enlivened
by the wide and cheerful windows of modern
times, which not only admit the light to animate the scene within, but also afford to the
spectator there, wide-spread, and sometimes en-
chanting views of the surrounding country.
The castle windows of ancient days were, on
the contrary, narrow loop-holes, each at the
bottom of a deep recess in the thick wall.   If
they had been made wide they would have admitted too easily the arrows and javelins of be-

siegers, as well as the wind and rain of wintery
storms. There were no books in these desolate
dwellings, no furniture but armor, no pleasures
but drinking and carousals.

Nor could these noble and valiant knights
and barons occupy themselves in any useful
employment. There was nothing which it was
respectable for them to do but to fight. They
looked down with contempt upon all the industrial pursuits of life. The cultivation of farms,
the rearing of flocks and herds, arts, manufac-
tures, and commerce—every thing of this sort,
by which man can benefit his fellow-man, was
entirely beneath them. In fact, their descendants to the present day, even in England, entertain the same ideas. Their younger sons can
enter the army or the navy, and spend their
lives in killing and destroying, or in awaiting,
in idleness, dissipation, and vice, for orders to
kill and destroy, without dishonor ; but to engage in any way in those vast and magnificent
operations of peaceful industry, on which the
true greatness and glory of England depend,
would be perpetual and irretrievable disgrace.
A young nobleman can serve, in the most subordinate official capacity, on board a man-of-
war, and take pay for it, without degradation ;

but to *build* a man-of-war itself and take pay
for it, would be to compel his whole class to dis-
own him.

It was in consequence of this state of feeling
among the knights and barons of William's day
that peace was always tedious and irksome to
them, and they were never contented except
when engaged in battles and campaigns. It
was this feeling, probably, quite as much as
any settled hostility to William's right to reign,
that made his barons so eager to engage in insurrections and rebellions. There was, however, after all, a real and deep-seated opposition
to William's right of succession, founded in the
ideas of the day. They could not well endure
that one of so humble and even ignominious
birth, on the mother's side, should be the heir
of so illustrious a line as the great dukes of
Normandy. William's enemies were accustomed to designate him by opprobrious epithets,
derived from the circumstances of his birth.
Though he was patient and enduring, and often
very generous in forgiving other injuries, these
insults to the memory of his mother always
stung him very deeply, and awakened the
strongest emotions of resentment. One instance of this was so conspicuous that it is re-

corded in almost all the histories of William
that have been written.

It was in the midst of one of the wars in
which he was involved, that he was advancing
across the country to the attack of a strong
castle, which, in addition to the natural strength
of its walls and fortifications, was defended by
a numerous and powerful garrison. So confident, in fact, were the garrison in their numbers and power, that when they heard that
William was advancing to attack them, they
sent out a detachment to meet him. This detachment, however, were not intending to give
him open battle. Their plan was to lay in
ambuscade, and attack William's troops when
they came to the spot, and while they were un-
aware of the vicinity of an enemy, and off their
guard.

William, however, they found, was not off his
guard. He attacked the ambuscade with so
much vigor as to put the whole force immediately to flight. Of course the fugitives directed their steps toward the castle. William and
his soldiers followed them in headlong pursuit.
The end was, that the detachment from the garrison had scarcely time, after making good their
own entrance, to raise the draw-bridges and se-

cure the gates, so as to keep their pursuers from entering too. They did, however, succeed in doing this, and William, establishing his troops about the castle, opened his lines and commenced a regular siege.

The garrison were very naturally vexed and irritated at the bad success of their intended stratagem. To have the ambuscade not only fail of its object, but to have also the men that formed it driven thus ignominiously in, and so narrowly escaping, also, the danger of letting in the whole troop of their enemies after them, was a great disgrace. To retaliate upon William, and to throw back upon him the feelings of mortification and chagrin which they felt themselves, they mounted the walls and towers, and shouted out all sorts of reproaches and insults. Finally, when they found that they could not make mere words sufficiently stinging, they went and procured skins and hides, and aprons of leather, and every thing else that they could find that was connected with the trade of a tanner, and shook them at the troops of their assailants from the towers and walls, with shouts of merriment and derision.

William was desperately enraged at these insults. He organized an assaulting party, and

by means of the great exertions which the exasperation of his men stimulated them to make,
he carried some of the outworks, and took a
number of prisoners. These prisoners he cut
to pieces, and then caused their bloody and
mangled limbs and members to be thrown, by
great slings, over the castle walls.

At one time during the period which is in-
cluded within the limits of this chapter, and in
the course of one of those intervals of peace and
quietness within his own dominions which William sometimes enjoyed, the King of France became involved in a war with one of his own rebellious subjects, and William went, with an
army of Normans, to render him aid. King
Henry was at first highly gratified at this
prompt and effectual succor, but he soon afterward began to feel jealous of the universal pop-
ularity and renown which the young duke began soon to acquire. William was at that time
only about twenty-four years old, but he took
the direction of every thing—moved to and fro
with the utmost celerity—planned the campaigns—directed the sieges, and by his personal
accomplishments and his bravery, he won all
hearts, and was the subject of every body's
praises. King Henry found himself supplant-

ed, in some measure, in the regard and honorable consideration of his subjects, and he began to feel very envious and jealous of his rival.

Sometimes particular incidents would occur, in which William's feats of prowess or dexterity would so excite the admiration of the army that he would be overwhelmed with acclamations and applause. These were generally exploits of combat on the field, or of escape from pursuers when outnumbered, in which good fortune had often, perhaps, quite as much to do in securing the result as strength or courage. But in those days a soldier's good luck was perhaps as much the subject of applause as his muscular force or his bravery; and, in fact, it was as deservedly so; for the strength of arm, and the coolness, or, rather, the ferocity of courage, which make a good combatant in personal contests on a battle-field, are qualities of brutes rather than of men. We feel a species of respect for them in the lion or tiger, but they deserve only execration when exercised in the wantonness of hatred and revenge by man against his brother man.

One of the instances of William's extraordinary success was the following. He was reconnoitering the enemy on one occasion, ac-

companied only by four or five knights, who
acted as his attendants and body-guard. The
party were at a distance from the camp of the
enemy, and supposed they were not observed.
They were observed, however, and immediately
a party of twelve chosen horsemen was formed,
and ordered to ride out and surprise them. This
detachment concealed themselves in an ambuscade, at a place where the reconnoitering party
must pass, and when the proper moment arrived, they burst out suddenly upon them and
summoned them to surrender. Twelve against
six seemed to render both flight and resistance
equally vain. William, however, advanced immediately to the attack of the ambuscaders. He
poised his long lance, and, riding on with it at
full speed, he unhorsed and killed the foremost
of them at a blow. Then, just drawing back
his weapon to gather strength for another blow,
he killed the second of his enemies in the same
manner. His followers were so much animated
at this successful onset, that they advanced very
resolutely to the combat. In the mean time,
the shouts carried the alarm to William's camp,
and a strong party set off to rescue William
and his companions. The others then turned
to fly, while William followed them so eagerly

and closely, that he and they who were with him overtook and disabled seven of them, and made them prisoners. The rest escaped. William and his party then turned and began to proceed toward their own camp, conveying their prisoners in their train.

They were met by King Henry himself at the head of a detachment of three hundred men, who, not knowing how much necessity there might be for efficient aid, were hastening to the scene of action. The sight of William coming home victorious, and the tales told by his companions of the invincible strength and daring which he had displayed in the sudden danger, awakened a universal enthusiasm, and the plaudits and encomiums with which the whole camp resounded were doubtless as delicious and intoxicating to him as they were bitter to the king.

It was by such deeds, and by such personal and mental characteristics as these, that William, notwithstanding the untoward influences of his birth, fought his way, during the twenty years of which we have been speaking, into general favor, and established a universal renown. He completely organized and arranged the internal affairs of his own kingdom, and established himself firmly upon the ducal throne. His mind had become mature, his resources were well developed, and his soul, always ambitious and aspiring, began to reach forward to the grasping of some grander objects of pursuit, and to the entering upon some wider field of action than his duchy of Normandy could afford. During this interval, however, he was married; and, as the circumstances of his marriage were somewhat extraordinary, we must make that event the subject of a separate chapter.

CHAPTER V.

THE MARRIAGE.

ONE of the most important points which an hereditary potentate has to attend to, in completing his political arrangements, is the question of his marriage. Until he has a family and an heir, men's minds are unsettled in respect to the succession, and the various rival candidates and claimants to the throne are perpetually plotting and intriguing to put themselves into a position to spring at once into his place if sickness, or a battle, or any sudden accident should take him away. This evil was more formidable than usual in the case of William, for the men who were prepared to claim his place when he was dead were all secretly or openly maintaining that their right to it was superior to his while he was living. This gave a double intensity to the excitement with which the public was perpetually agitated in respect to the crown, and kept the minds of the ambitious and the aspiring, throughout William's dominions, in a continual fever. It was ob-

vious that a great part of the cause of this restless looking for change and consequent planning
to promote it would be removed if William had
a son.

It became, therefore, an important matter of
state policy that the duke should be married.
In fact, the barons and military chieftains who
were friendly to him urged this measure upon
him, on account of the great effect which they
perceived it would have in settling the minds
of the people of the country and consolidating
his power.   William accordingly began to look
around for a wife.   It appeared, however, in
the end, that, though policy was the main consideration which first led him to contemplate
marriage, love very probably exercised an important influence in determining his choice of
the lady ; at all events, the object of his choice
was an object worthy of love.   She was one of
the most beautiful and accomplished princesses
in Europe.

She was the daughter of a great potentate
who ruled over the country of Flanders.   Flanders lies upon the coast, east of Normandy, beyond the frontiers of France, and on the southern shore of the German Ocean.   Her father's
title was the Earl of Flanders.   He governed

his dominions, however, like a sovereign, and
was at the head of a very effective military power.   His family, too, occupied a very high rank,
and enjoyed great consideration among the other
princes and potentates of Europe.   It had in-
termarried with the royal family of England,
so that Matilda, the daughter of the earl, whom
William was disposed to make his bride, was
found, by the genealogists, who took great interest in those days in tracing such connections,
to have descended in a direct line from the great
English king, Alfred himself.

This relationship, by making Matilda's birth
the more illustrious, operated strongly in favor
of the match, as a great part of the motive
which William had in view, in his intended
marriage, was to aggrandize and strengthen
his own position, by the connection which he
was about to form.   There was, however, another consanguinity in the case which had a
contrary tendency.   Matilda's father had been
connected with the Norman as well as with
the English line, and Matilda and William were
in some remote sense cousins.   This circumstance led, in the sequel, as will presently be
seen, to serious difficulty and trouble.

Matilda was seven years younger than Will-

iam. She was brought up in her father's court,
and famed far and wide for her beauty and accomplishments. The accomplishments in which
ladies of high rank sought to distinguish themselves in those days were two, music and embroidery. The embroidery of tapestry was the
great attainment, and in this art the young
Matilda acquired great skill. The tapestry
which was made in the Middle Ages was used
to hang against the walls of some of the more
ornamented rooms in royal palaces and castles,
to hide the naked surface of the stones of which
the building was constructed. The cloths thus
suspended were at first plain, afterward they
began to be ornamented with embroidered bor-
ders or other decorations, and at length ladies
learned to employ their own leisure hours, and
beguile the tedium of the long confinement
which many of them had to endure within their
castles, in embroidering various devices and designs on the hangings intended for their own
chambers, or to execute such work as presents
for their friends. Matilda's industry and skill
in this kind of work were celebrated far and
wide.

The accomplishments which ladies take great
pains to acquire in their early years are some-

times, it is said, laid almost entirely aside after their marriage ; not necessarily because they are then less desirous to please, but sometimes from the abundance of domestic duty, which allows them little time, and sometimes from the pressure of their burdens of care or sorrow, which leave them no heart for the occupations of amusement or gayety. It seems not to have been so in Matilda's case, however. She resumed her needle often during the years of her wedded life, and after William had accomplished his conquest of England, she worked upon a long linen web, with immense labor, a series of designs illustrating the various events and incidents of his campaign, and the work has been preserved to the present day.

At least there is such a web now existing in the ancient town of Bayeux, in Normandy. which has been there from a period beyond the memory of men, and which tradition says was worked by Matilda. It would seem, however, that if she did it at all, she must have done it " as Solomon built the temple—with a great deal of help ;" for this famous piece of embroidery, which has been celebrated among all the historians and scholars of the world for several hundred years by the name of the *Bayeux Tap-*

estry, is over four hundred feet long, and nearly two feet wide. The web is of linen, while the embroidery is of woolen. It was all obviously executed with the needle, and was worked with infinite labor and care. The woolen thread which was used was of various colors, suited to represent the different objects in the design, though these colors are, of course, now much tarnished and faded.

The designs themselves are very simple and even rude, evincing very little knowledge of the principles of modern art. The specimens on the following page, of engravings made from them, will give some idea of the childish style of delineation which characterizes all Matilda's designs. Childish, however, as such a style of drawing would be considered now, it seems to have been, in Matilda's days, very much praised and admired.

We often have occasion to observe, in watching the course of human affairs, the frailty and transitoriness of things apparently most durable and strong. In the case of this embroidery, on the contrary, we are struck with the durability and permanence of what would seem to be most frail and fleeting. William's conquest of England took place in 1066. This piece of tapes-

Specimens of the designs of the Bayeux tapestry.

PLOWING. From the Bayeux tapestry.

SOWING. From the Bayeux tapestry.

try, therefore, if Matilda really worked it, is about eight hundred years old. And when we consider how delicate, slender, and frail is the fibre of a linen thread, and that the various elements of decay, always busy in the work of corrupting and destroying the works of man, have proved themselves powerful enough to waste away and crumble into ruin the proudest structures which he has ever attempted to rear, we are amazed that these slender filaments have been able to resist their action so long. The Bayeux tapestry has lasted nearly a thousand years. It will probably last for a thousand years to come. So that the vast and resistless power, which destroyed Babylon and Troy, and is making visible progress in the work of destroying the Pyramids, is foiled by the durability of a piece of needle-work, executed by the frail and delicate fingers of a woman.

We may have occasion to advert to the Bayeux tapestry again, when we come to narrate the exploits which it was the particular object of this historical embroidery to illustrate and adorn. In the mean time, we return to our story.

The matrimonial negotiations of princes and princesses are always conducted in a formal and ceremonious manner, and through the intervention of legates, embassadors, and commissioners without number, who are, of course, interested in protracting the proceedings, so as to prolong, as much as possible, their own diplomatic importance and power. Besides these accidental and temporary difficulties, it soon appeared that there were, in this case, some real and very formidable obstacles, which threatened for a time entirely to frustrate the scheme.

Among these difficulties there was one which was not usually, in such cases, considered of much importance, but which, in this instance, seemed for a long time to put an effectual bar to William's wishes, and that was the aversion which the young princess herself felt for the match. She could have, one would suppose, no personal feeling of repugnance against William, for he was a tall and handsome cavalier, highly graceful and accomplished, and renowned for his bravery and success in war. He was, in every respect, such a personage as would be most likely to captivate the imagination of a maiden princess in those warlike times. Matilda, however, made objections to his birth. She could not consider him as the legitimate descendant and heir of the dukes of Normandy. It is true, he was then in possession of the

throne, but he was regarded by a large portion
of the most powerful chieftains in his realm as
a usurper. He was liable, at any time, on
some sudden change of fortune, to be expelled
from his dominions. His position, in a word,
though for the time being very exalted, was too
precarious and unstable, and his personal claims
to high social rank were too equivocal, to justify her trusting her destiny in his hands. In a
word, Matilda's answer to William's proposals
was an absolute refusal to become his wife.

These ostensible grounds, however, on which
Matilda based her refusal, plausible as they
were, were not the real and true ones. The
secret motive was another attachment which
she had formed. There had been sent to her
father's court in Flanders, from the English
king, a young Saxon embassador, whose name
was Brihtric. Brihtric remained some little
time at the court in Flanders, and Matilda,
who saw him often at the various entertainments, celebrations, and parties of pleasure
which were arranged for his amusement, conceived a strong attachment to him. He was
of a very fair complexion, and his features were
expressive and beautiful. He was a noble of
high position in England, though, of course, his

rank was inferior to that of Matilda. As it would have been deemed hardly proper for him, under the circumstances of the case, to have aspired to the princess's hand, on account of the superiority of her social position, Matilda felt that it was her duty to make known her sentiments to him, and thus to open the way. She did so; but she found, unhappy maiden, that Brihtric did not feel, himself, the love which he had inspired in her, and all the efforts and arts to which she was impelled by the instinct of affection proved wholly unavailing to call it forth. Brihtric, after fulfilling the object of his mission, took leave of Matilda coldly, while *her* heart was almost breaking, and went away.

As the sweetest wine transforms itself into the sharpest vinegar, so the warmest and most ardent love turns, when it turns at all, to the most bitter and envenomed hate. Love gave place soon in Matilda's heart to indignation, and indignation to a burning thirst for revenge. The intensity of the first excitement subsided; but Matilda never forgot and never forgave the disappointment and the indignity which she had endured. She had an opportunity long afterward to take terrible revenge on Brihtric

A.D. 1045–52.] THE MARRIAGE. 107

William and Matilda's consanguinity.   An obstacle to their marriage

in England, by subjecting him to cruelties and
hardships there which brought him to his grave.

In the mean time, while her thoughts were
so occupied with this attachment, she had, of
course, no heart to listen favorably to William's proposals. Her friends would have attached no importance to the real cause of her
aversion to the match, but they felt the force
of the objections which could justly be advanced
against William's rank, and his real right to
his throne. Then the consanguinity of the
parties was a great source of embarrassment
and trouble. Persons as nearly related to each
other as they were, were forbidden by the Roman Catholic rules to marry. There was such
a thing as getting a dispensation from the pope,
by which the marriage would be authorized.
William accordingly sent embassadors to Rome
to negotiate this business. This, of course,
opened a new field for difficulties and delays.

The papal authorities were accustomed, in
such cases, to exact as the price, or, rather, as
the condition of their dispensation, some grant
or beneficial conveyance from the parties interested, to the Church, such as the foundation of
an abbey or a monastery, the building of a
chapel, or the endowment of a charity, by way,

as it were, of making amends to the Church, by
the benefit thus received, for whatever injury
the cause of religion and morality might sus-
tain by the relaxation of a divine law. Of
course, this being the end in view, the tendency
on the part of the authorities at Rome would
be to protract the negotiations, so as to obtain
from the suitor's impatience better terms in the
end. The embassadors and commissioners, too,
on William's part, would have no strong motive
for hastening the proceedings. Rome was an
agreeable place of residence, and to live there as
the embassador of a royal duke of Normandy
was to enjoy a high degree of consideration, and
to be surrounded continually by scenes of magnificence and splendor. Then, again, William
himself was not always at leisure to urge the
business forward by giving it his own close attention; for, during the period while these negotiations were pending, he was occupied, from
time to time, with foreign wars, or in the sup-
pression of rebellions among his barons. Thus,
from one cause and another, it seemed as if the
business would never come to an end.

In fact, a less resolute and determined man
than William would have given up in despair,
for it was seven years, it is said, before the af-

fair was brought to a conclusion. One story is told of the impetuous energy which William manifested in this suit, which seems almost incredible.

It was after the negotiations had been protracted for several years, and at a time when the difficulties were principally those arising from Matilda's opposition, that the occurrence took place. It was at an interview which William had with Matilda in the streets of Bruges, one of her father's cities. All that took place at the interview is not known, but in the end of it William's resentment at Matilda's treatment of him lost all bounds. He struck her or pushed her so violently as to throw her down upon the ground. It is said that he struck her repeatedly, and then, leaving her with her clothes all soiled and disheveled, rode off in a rage. Love quarrels are often the means of bringing the contending parties nearer together than they were before, but such a terrible love quarrel as this, we hope, is very rare.

Violent as it was, however, it was followed by a perfect reconciliation, and in the end all obstacles were removed, and William and Matilda were married. The event took place in 1052.

The marriage ceremony was performed at
one of William's castles, on the frontiers of Normandy, as it is customary for princes and kings
to be married always in their own dominions.
Matilda was conducted there with great pomp
and parade by her parents, and was accompanied by a large train of attendants and friends.
This company, mounted—both knights and ladies—on horses beautifully caparisoned, moved
across the country like a little army on a march,
or rather like a triumphal procession escorting
a queen.   Matilda was received at the castle
with distinguished honor, and the marriage celebrations, and the entertainments accompany-
ing it, were continued for several days.   It was
a scene of unusual festivity and rejoicing.

The dress both of William and Matilda, on
this occasion, was very specially splendid. She
wore a mantle studded with the most costly
jewels; and, in addition to the other splendors
of his dress, William too wore a mantle and a
helmet, both of which were richly adorned with
the same costly decorations. So much importance was attached, in those days, to this outward show, and so great was the public interest taken in it, that these dresses of William
and Matilda, with all the jewelry that adorned

them, were deposited afterward in the great church at Bayeux, where they remained a sort of public spectacle, the property of the Church, for nearly five hundred years.

From the castle of Augi, where the marriage ceremonies were performed, William proceeded, after these first festivities and rejoicings were over, to the great city of Rouen, conducting his bride thither with great pomp and parade. Here the young couple established themselves, living in the enjoyment of every species of luxury and splendor which were attainable in those days. As has already been said, the interiors, even of royal castles and palaces, presented but few of the comforts and conveniences deemed essential to the happiness of a home in modern times. The European ladies of the present day delight in their suites of retired and well-furnished apartments, adorned with velvet carpets, and silken curtains, and luxuriant beds of down, with sofas and couches adapted to every fancy which the caprice of fatigue or restlessness may assume, and cabinets stored with treasures, and libraries of embellished books—the whole scene illuminated by the splendor of gas-lights, whose brilliancy is reflected by mirrors and candelabras, sparkling with a thousand hues. Matil-

da's feudal palace presented no such scenes as
these. The cold stone floors were covered with
mats of rushes. The walls—if the naked masonry was hidden at all — were screened by
hangings of coarse tapestry, ornamented with
uncouth and hideous figures. The beds were
miserable pallets, the windows were loop-holes,
and the castle itself had all the architectural
characteristics of a prison.

Still, there was a species of luxury and splendor even then. Matilda had splendid horses to
ride, all magnificently caparisoned. She had
dresses adorned most lavishly with gold and
jewels. There were troops of valiant knights,
all glittering in armor of steel, to escort her on
her journeys, and accompany and wait upon
her on her excursions of pleasure; and there
were grand banquets and carousals, from time
to time, in the long castle hall, with tourna-
ments, and races, and games, and other military
shows, conducted with great parade and pa-
geantry. Matilda thus commenced her married
life in luxury and splendor.

In luxury and splendor, but not in peace.
William had an uncle, whose name was Mauger. He was the Archbishop of Rouen, and was
a dignitary of great influence and power. Now

it was, of course, the interest of William's relatives that he should not be married, as every increase of probability that his crown would descend to direct heirs diminished their future chances of the succession, and of course undermined their present importance. Mauger had been very much opposed to this match, and had exerted himself in every way, while the negotiations were pending, to impede and delay them. The point which he most strenuously urged was the consanguinity of the parties, a point to which it was incumbent on him, as he maintained—being the head of the Church in Normandy—particularly to attend. It seems that, notwithstanding William's negotiations with the pope to obtain a dispensation, the affair was not fully settled at Rome before the marriage; and very soon after the celebration of the nuptials, Mauger fulminated an edict of excommunication against both William and Matilda, for intermarrying within the degrees of relationship which the canons of the Church proscribed.

An excommunication, in the Middle Ages, was a terrible calamity. The person thus condemned was made, so far as such a sentence could effect it, an outcast from man, and a wretch accursed of Heaven. The most terrible

28—8

denunciations were uttered against him, and in the case of a prince, like that of William, his subjects were all absolved from their allegiance, and forbidden to succor or defend him. A powerful potentate like William could maintain himself for a time against the influence and effects of such a course, but it was pretty sure to work more and more strongly against him through the superstitions of the people, and to wear him out in the end.

William resolved to appeal at once to the pope, and to effect, by some means or other, the object of securing his dispensation. There was a certain monk, then obscure and unknown, but who afterward became a very celebrated public character, named Lanfranc, whom, for some reason or other, William supposed to possess the necessary qualifications for this mission. He accordingly gave him his instructions and sent him away. Lanfranc proceeded to Rome, and there he managed the negotiation with the pope so dexterously as soon to bring it to a conclusion.

The arrangement which he made was this. The pope was to grant the dispensation and confirm the marriage, thus removing the sentence of excommunication which the Archbish-

op Mauger had pronounced, on condition that
William should build and endow a hospital for
a hundred poor persons, and also erect two abbeys, one to be built by himself, for monks, and
one by Matilda, for nuns.   Lanfranc agreed to
these conditions on the part of William and
Matilda, and they, when they came to be informed of them, accepted and confirmed them
with great joy.   The ban of excommunication
was removed ; all Normandy acquiesced in the
marriage, and William and Matilda proceeded
to form the plans and to superintend the con-
struction of the abbeys.

They selected the city of Caen for the site.
The place of this city will be seen marked upon
the map near the northern coast of Normandy.*
It was situated in a broad and pleasant valley,
at the confluence of two rivers, and was surrounded by beautiful and fertile meadows.   It
was strongly fortified, being surrounded by walls
and towers, which William's ancestors, the
dukes of Normandy, had built.   William and
Matilda took a strong interest in the plans and
constructions connected with the building of
the abbeys.   William's was a very extensive
edifice, and contained within its inclosures a

* See map, chapter ix.

royal palace for himself, where, in subsequent
years, himself and Matilda often resided.

The principal buildings of these abbeys still
stand, though the walls and fortifications of
Caen are gone. The buildings are used now
for other purposes than those for which they
were erected, but they retain the names originally given them, and are visited by great numbers of tourists, being regarded with great interest as singular memorials of the past—twin
monuments commemorating an ancient marriage.

The marriage being thus finally confirmed
and acquiesced in, William and Matilda enjoyed a long period of domestic peace. The
oldest child was a son. He was born within a
year of the marriage, and William named him
Robert, that, as the reader will recollect, having been the name of William's father. There
was, in process of time, a large family of children. Their names were Robert, William Rufus, Henry, Cecilia, Agatha, Constance, Adela,
Adelaide, and Gundred. Matilda devoted herself with great maternal fidelity to the care and
education of these children, and many of them
became subsequently historical personages of
the highest distinction.

The object which, it will be recollected, was one of William's main inducements for contracting this alliance, namely, the strengthening of his power by thus connecting himself with the reigning family of Flanders, was, in a great measure, accomplished. The two governments, leagued together by this natural tie, strengthened each other's power, and often rendered each other essential assistance, though there was one occasion, subsequently, when William's reliance on this aid was disappointed. It was as follows:

When he was planning his invasion of England, he sent to Matilda's brother, Baldwin, who was then Count of Flanders, inviting him to raise a force and join him. Baldwin, who considered the enterprise as dangerous and Quixotic, sent back word to inquire what share of the English territory William would give him if he would go and help him conquer it. William thought that this attempt to make a bargain beforehand, for a division of spoil, evinced a very mercenary and distrustful spirit on the part of his brother-in-law—a spirit which he was not at all disposed to encourage. He accordingly took a sheet of parchment, and writing nothing within, he folded it in the form of a letter, and wrote upon the outside the following rhyme :

> "Beau frère, en Angleterre vous aures
> Ce qui dedans escript, vous trouveres."

Which royal distich might be translated thus :

> "Your share, good brother, of the land we win,
> You'll find entitled and described within."

William forwarded the empty missive by the hand of a messenger, who delivered it to Baldwin as if it were a dispatch of great consequence. Baldwin received it eagerly, and opened it at once. He was surprised at finding nothing within ; and after turning the parchment every way, in vain search after the description of his share, he asked the messenger what it meant "It means," said he, "that as there is nothing writ within, so nothing you shall have."

Notwithstanding this witticism, however, some arrangement seems afterward to have been made between the parties, for Flanders did, in fact, contribute an important share toward the force which William raised when preparing for the invasion.

A.D. 1002.] THE LADY EMMA. 119

William's claims to the English throne.   The Lady Emma.

CHAPTER VI.

THE LADY EMMA.

IT is not to be supposed that, even in the war-like times of which we are writing, such a potentate as a duke of Normandy would invade a country like England, so large and powerful in comparison to his own, without some pretext. William's pretext was, that he himself was the legitimate successor to the English crown, and that the English king who possessed it at the time of his invasion was a usurper. In order that the reader may understand the nature and origin of this his claim, it is necessary to relate somewhat in full the story of the Lady Emma.

By referring to the genealogy of the Norman line of dukes contained in the second chapter of this volume, it will be seen that Emma was the daughter of the first Richard. She was celebrated in her early years for her great personal beauty. They called her *the Pearl of Normandy*.

She married, at length, one of the kings of England, whose name was Ethelred. England was at that time distracted by civil wars, waged between the two antagonist races of Saxons and Danes. There were, in fact, two separate dynasties or lines of kings, who were contending, all the time, for the mastery. In these contests, sometimes the Danes would triumph for a time, and sometimes the Saxons; and sometimes both races would have a royal representative in the field, each claiming the throne, and reigning over separate portions of the island. Thus there were, at certain periods, two kingdoms in England, both covering the same territory, and claiming the government of the same population—with two kings, two capitals, two administrations—while the wretched inhabitants were distracted and ruined by the terrible conflicts to which these hostile pretensions gave rise.

Ethelred was of the Saxon line. He was a widower at the time of his marriage to Emma, nearly forty years old, and he had, among other children by his former wife, a son named Edmund, an active, energetic young man, who afterward became king. One motive which he had in view in marrying Emma was to strengthen his position by securing the alliance of the Normans of Normandy. The Danes, his English enemies, were Normans. The government of Normandy would therefore be naturally inclined to take part with them. By this marriage, however, Ethelred hoped to detach the Normans of France from the cause of his enemies, and to unite them to his own. He would thus gain a double advantage, strengthening himself by an accession which weakened his foes.

His plan succeeded so far as inducing Richard himself, the Duke of Normandy, to espouse his cause, but it did not enable Ethelred to triumph over his enemies. They, on the contrary, conquered *him*, and, in the end, drove him from the country altogether. He fled to Normandy for refuge, with Emma his wife, and his two young sons. Their names were Edward and Alfred.

Richard II., Emma's brother, who was then the Duke of Normandy, received the unhappy fugitives with great kindness, although *he*, at least, scarcely deserved it. It was not surprising that he was driven from his native realm, for he possessed none of those high qualities of mind which fit men to conquer or to govern. Like all other weak-minded tyrants, he substituted cruelty for wisdom and energy in his attempts to subjugate his foes. As soon as he was married to Emma, for instance, feeling elated and strong at the great accession of power which he imagined he had obtained by this alliance, he planned a general massacre of the Danes, and executed it on a given day, by means of private orders, sent secretly throughout the kingdom. Vast numbers of the Danes were destroyed; and so great was the hatred of the two races for each other, that they who had these bloody orders to obey executed them with a savage cruelty that was absolutely horrible. In one instance they buried women to the waist, and then set dogs upon them, to tear their naked flesh until they died in agony. It would be best, in narrating history, to suppress such horrid details as these, were it not that in a land like this, where so much depends upon the influence of every individual in determining whether the questions and discussions which are from time to time arising, and are hereafter to arise, shall be settled peacefully, or by a resort to violence and civil war, it is very important that we should all know what civil war is, and to what horrible atrocities it inevitably leads.

Alfred the Great, when he was contending with the Danes in England, a century before this time, treated them, so far as he gained advantages over them, with generosity and kindness; and this policy wholly conquered them in

the end.   Ethelred, on the other hand, tried the
effect of the most tyrannical cruelty, and the
effect was only to arouse his enemies to a more
determined and desperate resistance.   It was
the phrensy of vengeance and hate that these
atrocities awakened every where among the
Danes, which nerved them with so much vigor
and strength that they finally expelled him from
the island; so that, when he arrived in Normandy, a fugitive and an exile, he came in the
character of a dethroned tyrant, execrated for
his senseless and atrocious cruelties, and not in
that of an unhappy prince driven from his home
by the pressure of unavoidable calamity.   Nevertheless, Richard, the Duke of Normandy, received him, as we have already said, with kindness.   He felt the obligation of receiving the
exiled monarch in a hospitable manner, if not
on his own account, at least for the sake of
Emma and the children.

The origin and end of Emma's interest in
Ethelred seems to have been merely ambition.
The "Pearl of Normandy" had given herself to
this monster for the sake, apparently, of the
glory of being the English queen.   Her subsequent conduct compels the readers of history to
make this supposition, which otherwise would

be uncharitable. She now mourned her disappointment in finding that, instead of being sustained by her husband in the lofty position to which she aspired, she was obliged to come back to her former home again, to be once more dependent, and with the additional burden of her husband himself, and her children, upon her father's family. Her situation was rendered even still more humiliating, in some degree, by the circumstances that her father was no longer alive, and that it was to her brother, on whom her natural claim was far less strong, that she had now to look for shelter and protection. Richard, however, received them all in a kind and generous manner.

In the mean time, the wars and commotions which had driven Ethelred away continued to rage in England, the Saxons gradually gaining ground against the Danes. At length the king of the Danes, who had seized the government when Ethelred was expelled, died. The Saxons then regained their former power, and they sent commissioners to Ethelred to propose his return to England. At the same time, they expressed their unwillingness to receive him, unless they could bind him, by a solemn treaty, to take a very different course of conduct, in the future

management of his government, from that which
he had pursued before. Ethelred and Emma
were eager to regain, on any terms, their lost
throne. They sent over embassadors empow-
ered to make, in Ethelred's name, any promises which the English nobles might demand;
and shortly afterward the royal pair crossed the
Channel and went to London, and Ethelred was
acknowledged there by the *Saxon* portion of
the population of the island once more as king.

The *Danes*, however, though weakened, were
not yet disposed to submit. They declared
their allegiance to *Canute*, who was the successor in the *Danish* line. Then followed a
long war between Canute and Ethelred. Canute was a man of extraordinary sagacity and
intelligence, and also of great courage and energy. Ethelred, on the other hand, proved himself, notwithstanding all his promises, incurably
inefficient, cowardly, and cruel. In fact, his
son Prince Edmund, the son of his first wife,
was far more efficient than his father in resist-
ing Canute and the Danes. Edmund was active and fearless, and he soon acquired very extensive power. In fact, he seems to have held
the authority of his father in very little respect.
One striking instance of this insubordination

occurred.   Ethelred had taken offense, for some reason or other, at one of the nobles in his realm, and had put him to death, and confiscated his estates ; and, in addition to this, with a cruelty characteristic of him, he shut up the unhappy widow of his victim, a young and beautiful woman, in a gloomy convent, as a prisoner. Edmund, his son, went to the convent, liberated the prisoner, and made her his own wife.

With such unfriendly relations between the king and his son, who seems to have been the ablest general in his father's army, there could be little hope of making head against such an enemy as Canute the Dane.   In fact, the course of public affairs went on from bad to worse, Emma leading all the time a life of unceasing anxiety and alarm.   At length, in 1016, Ethelred died, and Emma's cup of disappointment and humiliation was now full.   Her own sons, Edward and Alfred, had no claims to the crown ; for Edmund, being the son by a former marriage, was older than they.   They were too young to take personally an active part in the fierce contests of the day, and thus fight their way to importance and power.   And then Edmund, who was now to become king, would, of course, feel no interest in advancing *them*, or

THE RESCUE.

doing honor to *her*.   A son who would thwart
and counteract the plans and measures of a
father, as Edmund had done, would be little
likely to evince much deference or regard for a
mother-in-law, or for half brothers, whom he
would naturally consider as his rivals.   In a
word, Emma had reason to be alarmed at the
situation of insignificance and danger in which
she found herself suddenly placed.   She fled a
second time, in destitution and distress, to her
brother's in Normandy.   She was now, however, a widow, and her children were fatherless.
It is difficult to decide whether to consider her
situation as better or worse on this account,
than it was at her former exile.

Her sons were lads, but little advanced beyond the period of childhood; and Edward, the
eldest, on whom the duty of making exertions
to advance the family interests would first de-
volve, was of a quiet and gentle spirit, giving
little promise that he would soon be disposed
to enter vigorously upon military campaigns.
Edmund, on the other hand, who was now king,
was in the prime of life, and was a man of great
spirit and energy.   There was a reasonable
prospect that he would live many years; and
even if he were to be suddenly cut off, there

130   WILLIAM THE CONQUEROR.

War with Canute.   Treaty between Edmund and Canute.

seemed to be no hope of the restoration of Emma
to importance or power; for Edmund was married and had two sons, one of whom would be
entitled to succeed him in case of his decease.
It seemed, therefore, to be Emma's destiny now,
to spend the remainder of her days with her
children in neglect and obscurity.   The case
resulted differently, however, as we shall see in
the end.

Edmund, notwithstanding his prospect of a
long and prosperous career, was cut off suddenly, after a stormy reign of one year.   During
his reign, Canute the Dane had been fast gaining gronnd in England, notwithstanding the
vigor and energy with which Edmund had opposed him.   Finally, the two monarchs assembled their armies, and were about to fight a
great final battle.   Edmund sent a flag of truce
to Canute's camp, proposing that, to save the
effusion of blood, they should agree to decide
the case by single combat, and that he and Canute should be the champions, and fight in presence of the armies.   Canute declined this proposal.   He was himself small and slender in
form, while Edmund was distinguished for his
personal development and muscular strength.
Canute therefore declined the personal contest,

but offered to leave the question to the decision
of a council chosen from among the leading
nobles on either side. This plan was finally
adopted. The council convened, and, after long
deliberations, they framed a treaty by which the
country was divided between the two potentates, and a sort of peace was restored. A very
short period after this treaty was settled, Edmund was murdered.

Canute immediately laid claim to the whole
realm. He maintained that it was a part of
the treaty that the partition of the kingdom was
to continue only during their joint lives, and
that, on the death of either, the whole was to
pass to the survivor of them. The Saxon leaders did not admit this, but they were in no condition very strenuously to oppose it. Ethelred's
sons by Emma were too young to come forward
as leaders yet ; and as to Edmund's, they were
mere children. There was, therefore, no one
whom they could produce as an efficient representative of the Saxon line, and thus the Saxons were compelled to submit to Canute's pretensions, at least for a time. They would not
wholly give up the claims of Edmund's children,
but they consented to waive them for a season.
They gave Canute the guardianship of the boys

until they should become of age, and allowed
him, in the mean time, to reign, himself, over
the whole land.

Canute exercised his power in a very discreet
and judicious manner, seeming intent, in all
his arrangements, to protect the rights and interests of the Saxons as well as of the Danes.
It might be supposed that the lives of the young
Saxon princes, Edmund's sons, would not have
been safe in his hands; but the policy which he
immediately resolved to pursue was to conciliate the Saxons, and not to intimidate and coerce
them. He therefore did the young children no
harm, but sent them away out of the country to
Denmark, that they might, if possible, be gradually forgotten. Perhaps he thought that, if
the necessity should arise for it, they might
there, at any time, be put secretly to death.

There was another reason still to prevent
Canute's destroying these children, which was,
that if *they* were removed, the claims of the
Saxon line would not thereby be extinguished,
but would only be transferred to Emma's children in Normandy, who, being older, were likely the sooner to be in a condition to give him
trouble as rivals. It was therefore a very wise
and sagacious policy which prompted him to

keep the young children of Edmund alive, but
to remove them to a safe distance out of the way.

In respect to Emma's children, Canute conceived a different plan for guarding against any
danger which came from their claims, and that
was, to propose to take their mother for his wife.
By this plan her family would come into his
power, and then her own influence and that of
her Norman friends would be forever prevented
from taking sides against him. He accordingly made the proposal. Emma was ambitious
enough of again returning to her former position
of greatness as English queen to accept it eagerly. The world condemned her for being so
ready to marry, for her second husband, the
deadly enemy and rival of the first; but it was
all one to her whether her husband was Saxon
or Dane, provided that she could be queen.

The boys, or, rather, the young men, for they
were now advancing to maturity, were very
strongly opposed to this connection. They did
all in their power to prevent its consummation,
and they never forgave their mother for thus
basely betraying their interests. They were
the more incensed at this transaction, because
it was stipulated in the marriage articles between Canute and Emma that their *future* chil-

dren—the offspring of the marriage then con-
tracted—should succeed to the throne of England, to the exclusion of all previously born on
either side.   Thus Canute fancied that he had
secured his title, and that of his descendants, to
the crown forever, and Emma prepared to return to England as once more its queen.   The
marriage was celebrated with great pomp and
splendor, and Emma, bidding Normandy and
her now alienated children farewell, was conducted in state to the royal palace in London.

We must now pass over, with a very few
words, a long interval of twenty years.   It was
the period of Canute's reign, which was prosperous and peaceful.   During this period Emma's Norman sons continued in Normandy.
She had another son in England a few years
after her marriage, who was named Canute, after his father, but he is generally known in history by the name of Hardicanute, the prefix being a Saxon word denoting energetic or strong.
Canute had also a very celebrated minister in
his government named Godwin.   Godwin was
a Saxon of a very humble origin, and the history of his life constitutes quite a romantic tale.*

* It is given at length in the last chapter of our history
of Alfred the Great.

He was a man of extraordinary talents and character, and at the time of Canute's death he was altogether the most powerful subject in the realm.

When Canute found that he was about to die, and began to consider what arrangements he should make for the succession, he concluded that it would not be safe for him to fulfill the agreement made in his marriage contract with Emma, that the children of that marriage should inherit the kingdom; for Hardicanute, who was entitled to succeed under that covenant, was only about sixteen or seventeen years old, and consequently too young to attempt to govern. He therefore made a will, in which he left the kingdom to an older son, named Harold —a son whom he had had before his marriage with Emma. This was the signal for a new struggle. The influence of the Saxons and of Emma's friends was of course in favor of Hardicanute, while the Danes espoused the cause of Harold. Godwin at length taking sides with this last-named party, Harold was established on the throne, and Emma and all her children, whether descended from Ethelred or Canute, were set aside and forgotten.

Emma was not at all disposed to acquiesce

in this change of fortune.   She remained in
England, but was secretly incensed at her second husband's breach of faith toward her; and
as he had abandoned the child of his marriage
with her for *his* former children, she now determined to abandon him for *hers.*   She gave
up Hardicanute's cause, therefore, and began
secretly to plot among the Saxon population
for bringing forward her son Edward to the
throne.   When she thought that things were
ripe for the execution of the plot, she wrote a
letter to her children in Normandy, saying to
them that the Saxon population were weary of
the Danish line, and were ready, she believed,
to rise in behalf of the ancient Saxon line, if
the true representative of it would appear to
lead them.   She therefore invited them to come
to London and consult with her on the subject.
She directed them, however, to come, if they
came at all, in a quiet and peaceful manner,
and without any appearance of hostile intent,
inasmuch as any thing which might seem like
a foreign invasion would awaken universal jealousy and alarm.

When this letter was received by the brothers in Normandy, the eldest, Edward, declined
to go, but gave his consent that Alfred should

undertake the expedition if he were disposed. Alfred accepted the proposal. In fact, the temperament and character of the two brothers were very different. Edward was sedate, serious, and timid. Alfred was ardent and aspiring. The younger, therefore, decided to take the risk of crossing the Channel, while the elder preferred to remain at home.

The result was very disastrous. Contrary to his mother's instructions, Alfred took with him quite a troop of Norman soldiers. He crossed the Channel in safety, and advanced across the country some distance toward London. Harold sent out a force to intercept him. He was surrounded, and he himself and all his followers were taken prisoners. He was sentenced to lose his eyes, and he died in a few days after the execution of this terrible sentence, from the mingled effects of fever and of mental anguish and despair. Emma fled to Flanders.

Finally Harold died, and Hardicanute succeeded him. In a short time Hardicanute died, leaving no heirs, and now, of course, there was no one left* to compete with Emma's oldest

* The children of Ethelred's oldest son, Edmund, were in Hungary at this time, and seem to have been wellnigh forgotten.

son Edward, who had remained all this time
quietly in Normandy. He was accordingly proclaimed king. This was in 1041. He reigned
for twenty years, having commenced his reign
about the time that William the Conqueror was
established in the possession of his dominions as
Duke of Normandy. Edward had known William intimately during his long residence in Normandy, and William came to visit him in England in the course of his reign. William, in
fact, considered himself as Edward's heir; for
as Edward, though married, had no children,
the dukes of the Norman line were his nearest
relatives. He obtained, he said, a promise from
Edward that Edward would sanction and confirm his claim to the English crown, in the event
of his decease, by bequeathing it to William in
his will.

Emma was now advanced in years. The
ambition which had been the ruling principle
of her life would seem to have been well satisfied, so far as it is possible to satisfy ambition,
for she had had two husbands and two sons,
all kings of England. But as she advanced toward the close of her career, she found herself
wretched and miserable. Her son Edward
could not forgive her for her abandonment of

himself and his brother, to marry a man who
was their own and their father's bitterest enemy.
She had made a formal treaty in her marriage
covenant to exclude them from the throne.   She
had treated them with neglect during all the
time of Canute's reign, while she was living
with him in London in power and splendor.
Edward accused her, also, of having connived
at his brother Alfred's death.   The story is,
that he caused her to be tried on this charge
by the ordeal of fire.   This method consisted of
laying red-hot irons upon the stone floor of a
church, at certain distances from each other,
and requiring the accused to walk over them
with naked feet.   If the accused was innocent,
Providence, as they supposed, would so guide
his footsteps that he should not touch the irons.
Thus, if he was innocent, he would go over
safely ; if guilty, he would be burned.   Emma,
according to the story of the times, was sub-
jected to this test, in the Cathedral of Winchester, to determine whether she was cogni-
zant of the murder of her son.   Whether this
is true or not, there is no doubt that Edward
confined her a prisoner in the monastery at
Winchester, where she ended her days at last
in neglect and wretchedness.

When Edward himself drew near to the close of his life, his mind was greatly perplexed in respect to the succession. There was one descendant of his brother Edmund—whose children, it will be remembered, Canute had sent away to Denmark, in order to remove them out of the way—who was still living in Hungary. The name of this descendant was Edward. He was, in fact, the lawful heir to the crown. But he had spent his life in foreign countries, and was now far away; and, in the mean time, the Earl Godwin, who has been already mentioned as the great Saxon nobleman who rose from a very humble rank to the position of the most powerful subject in the realm, obtained such an influence, and wielded so great a power, that he seemed at one time stronger than the king himself. Godwin at length died, but his son Harold, who was as energetic and active as his father, inherited his power, and seemed, as Edward thought, to be aspiring to the future possession of the throne. Edward had hated Godwin and all his family, and was now extremely anxious to prevent the possibility of Harold's accession. He accordingly sent to Hungary to bring Edward, his nephew, home. Edward came, bringing his family with him. He had a young son named Edgar. It was King Edward's plan to make arrangements for bringing this Prince Edward to the throne after his death, that Harold might be excluded.

The plan was a very judicious one, but it was unfortunately frustrated by Prince Edward's death, which event took place soon after he arrived in England. The young Edgar, then a child, was, of course, his heir. The king was convinced that no government which could be organized in the name of Edgar would be able to resist the mighty power of Harold, and he turned his thoughts, therefore, again to the accession of William of Normandy, who was the nearest relative on his mother's side, as the only means of saving the realm from falling into the hands of the usurper Harold. A long and vexatious contest then ensued, in which the leading powers and influences of the kingdom were divided and distracted by the plans, plots, maneuvers, and counter maneuvers of Harold to obtain the accession for himself, and of Edward to secure it for William of Normandy. In this contest Harold conquered in the first instance, and Edward and William in the end.

142   WILLIAM THE CONQUEROR.

Harold and William.   Quarrel between Godwin and Edward.

CHAPTER VII.

KING HAROLD.

HAROLD, the son of the Earl Godwin, who was maneuvering to gain possession of the English throne, and William of Normandy, though they lived on opposite sides of the English Channel, the one in France and the other in England, were still personally known to each other; for not only had William, as was stated in the last chapter, paid a visit to England, but Harold himself, on one occasion, made an excursion to Normandy. The circumstances of this expedition were, in some respects, quite extraordinary, and illustrate in a striking manner some of the peculiar ideas and customs of the times. They were as follows:

During the life of Harold's father Godwin, there was a very serious quarrel between him, that is, Godwin, and King Edward, in which both the king and his rebellious subject marshaled their forces, and for a time waged against each other an open and sanguinary war. In this contest the power of Godwin had proved so formidable, and the military forces which he succeeded in marshaling under his banners were so great, that Edward's government was unable effectually to put him down.   At length, after a long and terrible struggle, which involved a large part of the country in the horrors of a civil war, the belligerents made a treaty with each other, which settled their quarrel by a sort of compromise.   Godwin was to retain his high position and rank as a subject, and to continue in the government of certain portions of the island which had long been under his jurisdiction; he, on his part, promising to dismiss his armies, and to make war upon the king no more.   He bound himself to the faithful performance of these covenants by giving the king *hostages*.

The hostages given up on such occasions were always near and dear relatives and friends, and the understanding was, that if the party giving them failed in fulfilling his obligations, the innocent and helpless hostages were to be entirely at the mercy of the other party into whose custody they had been given.   The latter would, in such cases, imprison them, torture them, or put them to death, with a greater or less degree of severity in respect to the infliction of pain, according to the degree of exasperation

which the real or fancied injury which he had
received awakened in his mind.

This cruel method of binding fierce and un-
principled men to the performance of their promises has been universally abandoned in modern
times, though in the rude and early stages of
civilization it has been practiced among all nations, ancient and modern. The hostages chosen were often of young and tender years, and
were always such as to render the separation
which took place when they were torn from
their friends most painful, as it was the very
object of the selection to obtain those who were
most beloved. They were delivered into the
hands of those whom they had always regarded
as their bitterest enemies, and who, of course,
were objects of aversion and terror. They were
sent away into places of confinement and seclu-
sion, and kept in the custody of strangers,
where they lived in perpetual fear that some
new outbreak between the contending parties
would occur, and consign them to torture or
death. The cruelties sometimes inflicted, in
such cases, on the innocent hostages, were awful. At one time, during the contentions between Ethelred and Canute, Canute, being driv-
en across the country to the sea-coast, and there

compelled to embark on board his ships to make
his escape, was cruel enough to cut off the hands
and the feet of some hostages which Ethelred
had previously given him, and leave them writh-
ing in agony on the sands of the shore.

The hostages which are particularly named
by historians as given by Godwin to King Edward were his son and his grandson. Their
names were Ulnoth and Hacune. Ulnoth, of
course, was Harold's brother, and Hacune his
nephew. Edward, thinking that Godwin would
contrive some means of getting these securities
back into his possession again if he attempted
to keep them in England, decided to send them
to Normandy, and to put them under the charge
of William the duke for safe keeping. When
Godwin died, Harold applied to Edward to give
up the hostages, since, as he alleged, there was
no longer any reason for detaining them. They
had been given as security for *Godwin's* good
behavior, and now Godwin was no more.

Edward could not well refuse to surrender
them, and yet, as Harold succeeded to the
power, and evidently possessed all the ambition
of his father, it seemed to be, politically, as
necessary to retain the hostages now as it had
been before. Edward, therefore, without abso-

28—10

lutely refusing to surrender them, postponed
and evaded compliance with Harold's demand,
on the ground that the hostages were in Normandy. He was going, he said, to send for
them as soon as he could make the necessary
arrangements for bringing them home in safety.

Under these circumstances, Harold determined to go and bring them himself. He proposed this plan to Edward. Edward would not
absolutely refuse his consent, but he did all in
his power to discourage such an expedition. He
told Harold that William of Normandy was a
crafty and powerful man; that by going into
his dominions he would put himself entirely
into his power, and would be certain to involve
himself in some serious difficulty. This interview between Harold and the king is commem-
orated on the Bayeux tapestry by the opposite
uncouth design.

What effect Edward's disapproval of the project produced upon Harold's mind is not cer-
tainly known. It is true that he went across
the Channel, but the accounts of the crossing
are confused and contradictory, some of them
stating that, while sailing for pleasure with a
party of attendants and companions on the coast,
he was blown off from the shore and driven

HAROLD'S INTERVIEW WITH EDWARD.

across to France by a storm.   The probability,
however, is, that this story was only a pretense.
He was determined to go, but not wishing to
act openly in defiance of the king's wishes, he
contrived to be blown off, in order to make it
seem that he went against his will.

At all events, the *storm* was real, whether
his being compelled to leave the English shores
by the power of it was real or pretended.   It

carried him, too, out of his course, driving him up the Channel to the eastward of Normandy, where he had intended to land, and at length throwing his galley, a wreck, on the shore, not far from the mouth of the Somme. The galley itself was broken up, but Harold and his company escaped to land. They found that they were in the dominions of a certain prince who held possessions on that coast, whose style and title was Guy, count of Ponthieu.

The law in those days was, that wrecks became the property of the lord of the territory on the shores of which they occurred; and not only were the ships and the goods which they contained thus confiscated in case of such a disaster, but the owners themselves became liable to be seized and held captive for a ransom. Harold, knowing his danger, was attempting to secrete himself on the coast till he could get to Normandy, when a fisherman who saw him, and knew by his dress and appearance, and by the deference with which he was treated by the rest of the company, that he was a man of great consequence in his native land, went to the count, and said that for ten crowns he would show him where there was a man who would be worth a thousand to him. The count came

down with his retinue to the coast, seized the un-
fortunate adventurers, took possession of all the
goods and baggage that the waves had spared,
and shut the men themselves up in his castle
at Abbeville till they could pay their ransom.

Harold remonstrated against this treatment.
He said that he was on his way to Normandy
on business of great importance with the duke,
from the King of England, and that he could
not be detained. But the count was very decided in refusing to let him go without his ransom. Harold then sent word to William, ac-
quainting him with his situation, and asking
him to effect his release. William sent to the
count, demanding that he should give his prisoner up. All these things, however, only tended to elevate and enlarge the count's ideas of
the value and importance of the prize which he
had been so fortunate to secure. He persisted
in refusing to give him up without ransom.
Finally William paid the ransom, in the shape
of a large sum of money, and the cession, in
addition, of a considerable territory. Harold
and his companions in bondage were then delivered to William's messengers, and conducted
by them in safety to Rouen, where William
was then residing.

10

William received his distinguished guest
with every possible mark of the most honorable
consideration. He was escorted with great parade and ceremony into the palace, lodged in
the most sumptuous manner, provided with every necessary supply, and games, and military
spectacles, and feasts and entertainments without number, were arranged to celebrate his visit.
William informed him that he was at liberty to
return to England whenever he pleased, and
that his brother and his nephew, the hostages
that he had come to seek, were at his disposal.
He, however, urged him not to return immediately, but to remain a short time in Normandy with his companions. Harold accepted the
invitation.

All this exuberance of hospitality had its origin, as the reader will readily divine, in the
duke's joy in finding the only important rival
likely to appear to contest his claims to the En-
lish crown so fully in his power, and in the
hope which he entertained of so managing affairs
at this visit as to divert Harold's mind from the
idea of becoming the King of England himself,
and to induce him to pledge himself to act in
his, that is, William's favor. He took, therefore, all possible pains to make him enjoy his

visit in Normandy; he exhibited to him the
wealth and the resources of the country—conducting him from place to place to visit the castles, the abbeys, and the towns—and, finally, he
proposed that he should accompany him on a
military expedition into Brittany.

Harold, pleased with the honors conferred
upon him, and with the novelty and magnificence of the scenes to which he was introduced,
entered heartily into all these plans, and his
companions and attendants were no less pleased
than he. William knighted many of these followers of Harold, and made them costly presents of horses, and banners, and suits of armor,
and other such gifts as were calculated to captivate the hearts of martial adventurers such as
they. William soon gained an entire ascendency over their minds, and when he invited
them to accompany him on his expedition into
Brittany, they were all eager to go.

Brittany was west of Normandy, and on the
frontiers of it, so that the expedition was not a
distant one. Nor was it long protracted. It
was, in fact, a sort of pleasure excursion, William taking his guest across the frontier into his
neighbor's territory, on a marauding party, just
as a nobleman, in modern times, would take a

party into a forest to hunt. William and Harold were on the most intimate and friendly terms possible during the continuance of this campaign. They occupied the same tent, and ate at the same table. Harold evinced great military talents and much bravery in the various adventures which they met with in Brittany, and William felt more than ever the desirableness of securing his influence on his, that is, William's side, or, at least, of preventing his becoming an open rival and enemy. On their return from Brittany into Normandy, he judged that the time had arrived for taking his measures. He accordingly resolved to come to an open understanding with Harold in respect to his plans, and to seek his co-operation.

He introduced the subject, the historians say, one day as they were riding along homeward from their excursion, and had been for some time talking familiarly on the way, relating tales to one another of wars, battles, sieges, and hair-breadth escapes, and other such adventures as formed, generally, the subjects of narrative conversation in those days. At length William, finding Harold, as he judged, in a favorable mood for such a communication, introduced the subject of the English realm and the approaching demise of the crown. He told him, confidentially, that there had been an arrange-ment between him, William, and King Ed-ward, for some time, that Edward was to *adopt* him as his successor. William told Harold, moreover, that he should rely a great deal on his co-operation and assistance in getting peace-able possession of the kingdom, and promised to bestow upon him the very highest rewards and honors in return if he would give him his aid. The only rival claimant, William said, was the young child Edgar, and he had no friends, no party, no military forces, and no means what-ever for maintaining his pretensions. On the other hand, he, William, and Harold, had obvi-ously all the power in their own hands, and if they could only co-operate together on a com-mon understanding, they would be sure to have the power and the honors of the English realm entirely at their disposal.

Harold listened to all these suggestions, and pretended to be interested and pleased. He was, in reality, interested, but he was not pleased. He wished to secure the kingdom for himself, not merely to obtain a share, however large, of its power and its honors as the subject of an-other. He was, however, too wary to evince his displeasure. On the contrary, he assented to the plan, professed to enter into it with all his heart, and expressed his readiness to commence, immediately, the necessary preliminary measures for carrying it into execution. William was much gratified with the successful result of his negotiation, and the two chieftains rode home to William's palace in Normandy, banded together, apparently, by very strong ties. In secret, however, Harold was resolving to effect his departure from Normandy as soon as possible, and to make immediate and most effectual measures for securing the kingdom of England to himself, without any regard to the promises that he had made to William.

Nor must it be supposed that William himself placed any positive reliance on mere promises from Harold. He immediately began to form plans for binding him to the performance of his stipulations, by the modes then commonly employed for securing the fulfillment of covenants made among princes. These methods were three—intermarriages, the giving of hostages, and solemn oaths.

William proposed two marriages as means of strengthening the alliance between himself and Harold. Harold was to give to William

one of his daughters, that William might marry
her to one of his Norman chieftains. This
would be, of course, placing her in William's
power, and making her a hostage all but in
name. Harold, however, consented. The second marriage proposed was between William's
daughter and Harold himself; but as his daughter was a child of only seven years of age, it
could only be a betrothment that could take
place at that time. Harold acceded to this
proposal too, and arrangements were made for
having the faith of the parties pledged to one
another in the most solemn manner. A great
assembly of all the knights, nobles, and ladies
of the court was convened, and the ceremony
of pledging the troth between the fierce warrior
and the gentle and wondering child was performed with as much pomp and parade as if it
had been an actual wedding. The name of the
girl was Adela.

In respect to hostages, William determined to
detain one of those whom Harold, as will be recollected, had come into Normandy to recover.
He told him, therefore, that he might take with
him his nephew Hacune, but that Ulnoth, his
brother, should remain, and William would
bring him over himself when he came to take

possession of the kingdom. Harold was extremely unwilling to leave his brother thus in
William's power; but as he knew very well that
his being allowed to return to England himself
would depend upon his not evincing any reluc-
tance to giving William security, or manifest-
ing any other indication that he was not intending to keep his plighted faith, he readily consented, and it was thus settled that Ulnoth
should remain.

Finally, in order to hold Harold to the fulfillment of his promises by every possible form of
obligation, William proposed that he should
take a public and solemn oath, in the presence
of a large assembly of all the great potentates
and chieftains of the realm, by which he should
bind himself, under the most awful sanctions, to
keep his word. Harold made no objection to
this either. He considered himself as, in fact,
in duress, and his actions as not free. He was
in William's power, and was influenced in all
he did by a desire to escape from Normandy,
and once more recover his liberty. He accordingly decided, in his own mind, that whatever
oaths he might take he should afterward consider as forced upon him, and consequently as
null and void, and was ready, therefore, to take
any that William might propose.

The great assembly was accordingly convened.   In the middle of the council hall there was
placed a great chair of state, which was covered
with a cloth of gold.   Upon this cloth, and raised considerably above the seat, was the *missal*,
that is, the book of service of the Catholic
Church, written on parchment and splendidly
illuminated.   The book was open at a passage
from one of the Evangelists—the Evangelists
being a portion of the Holy Scriptures which
was, in those days, supposed to invest an oath
with the most solemn sanctions.

Harold felt some slight misgivings as he advanced in the midst of such an imposing scene
as the great assembly of knights and ladies presented in the council hall, to repeat his promises in the very presence of God, and to impre-
cate the retributive curses of the Almighty on
the violation of them, which he was deliberately
and fully determined to incur.   He had, however, gone too far to retreat now.   He advanced, therefore, to the open missal, laid his hand
upon the book, and, repeating the words which
William dictated to him from his throne, he
took the threefold oath required, namely, to
aid William to the utmost of his power in his
attempt to secure the succession to the English

crown, to marry William's daughter Adela as
soon as she should arrive at a suitable age, and
to send over forthwith from England his own
daughter, that she might be espoused to one of
William's nobles.

As soon as the oath was thus taken, William
caused the missal and the cloth of gold to be removed, and there appeared beneath it, on the
chair of state, a chest, containing the sacred relics of the Church, which William had secretly
collected from the abbeys and monasteries of
his dominions, and placed in this concealment,
that, without Harold's being conscious of it,
their dreadful sanction might be added to that
which the Holy Evangelists imposed.   These
relics were fragments of bones set in caskets
and frames, and portions of blood—relics, as the
monks alleged, of apostles or of the Savior—and
small pieces of wood, similarly preserved, which
had been portions of the cross of Christ or of
his thorny crown.   These things were treasured
up with great solemnity in the monastic establishments and in the churches of these early
times, and were regarded with a veneration and
awe, of which it is almost beyond our power
even to conceive.   Harold trembled when he
saw what he had unwittingly done.   He was

terrified to think how much more dreadful was
the force of the imprecations that he had uttered than he had imagined while uttering them.
But it was too late to undo what he had done.
The assembly was finally dismissed.   William
thought he had the conscience of his new ally
firmly secured, and Harold began to prepare for
leaving Normandy.

He continued on excellent terms with William until his departure.   William accompanied
him to the sea-shore when the time of his embarkation arrived, and dismissed him at last
with many farewell honors, and a profusion of
presents.   Harold set sail, and, crossing the
Channel in safety, he landed in England.

He commenced immediately an energetic system of measures to strengthen his own cause,
and prepare the way for his own accession.   He
organized his party, collected arms and munitions of war, and did all that he could to ingrati-
ate himself with the most powerful and wealthy
nobles.   He sought the favor of the king, too,
and endeavored to persuade him to discard William.   The king was now old and infirm, and
was growing more and more inert and gloomy
as he advanced in age.   His mind was occupied altogether in ecclesiastical rites and ob-

servances, or plunged in a torpid and lifeless melancholy, which made him averse to giving any thought to the course which the affairs of his kingdom were to take after he was gone. He did not care whether Harold or William took the crown when he laid it aside, provided they would allow him to die in peace.

He had had, a few years previous to this time, a plan of making a pilgrimage to Jerusalem, but had finally made an arrangement with the pope, allowing him to build a Cathedral church, to be dedicated to St. Peter, a few miles west of London, in lieu of his pilgrimage. There was already a Cathedral church or *minster* in the heart of London which was dedicated to St. Paul. The new one was afterward often called, to distinguish it from the other, the *west* minster, which designation, Westminster, became afterward its regular name. It was on this spot, where Westminster Abbey now stands, that Edward's church was to be built. It was just completed at the time of which we are speaking, and the king was preparing for the dedication of it. He summoned an assembly of all the prelates and great ecclesiastical dignitaries of the land to convene at London, in order to dedicate the new Cathedral. Before they were

ready for the service, the king was taken suddenly sick.   They placed him upon his couch
in his palace chamber, where he lay, restless,
and moaning in pain, and repeating incessantly,
half in sleep and half in delirium, the gloomy
and threatening texts of Scripture which seemed to haunt his mind.   He was eager to have
the dedication go on, and they hastened the
service in order to gratify him by having it performed before he died.   The next day he was
obviously failing.   Harold and his friends were
very earnest to have the departing monarch declare in *his* favor before he died, and their coming
and going, and their loud discussions, rude soldiers as they were, disturbed his dying hours.
He sent them word to choose whom they would
for king, duke or earl, it was indifferent to him,
and thus expired.

Harold had made his arrangements so well,
and had managed so effectually to secure the
influence of all the powerful nobles of the kingdom, that they immediately convened and offered him the crown.   Edgar was in the court of
Edward at the time, but he was too young to
make any effort to advance his claims.   He
was, in fact, a foreigner, though in the English
royal line.   He had been brought up on the

Continent of Europe, and could not even speak
the English tongue. He acquiesced, therefore,
without complaint, in these proceedings, and
was even present as a consenting spectator on
the occasion of Harold's coronation, which ceremony was performed with great pomp and parade, at St. Paul's, in London, very soon after
King Edward's death. Harold rewarded Edgar for his complaisance and discretion by con-
ferring upon him the honor of knighthood immediately after the coronation, and in the church
where the ceremony was performed. He also
conferred similar distinctions and honors upon
many other aspiring and ambitious men whom
he wished to secure to his side. He thus seemed to have secure and settled possession of the
throne.

Previously to this time, Harold had married
a young lady of England, a sister of two very
powerful noblemen, and the richest heiress in
the realm. This marriage greatly strengthened his influence in England, and helped to prepare the way for his accession to the supreme
power. The tidings of it, however, when they
crossed the Channel and reached the ears of
William of Normandy, as the act was an open
and deliberate violation of one of the covenants

Harold violates his plighted faith to William.

which Harold had made with William, convinced the latter that none of these covenants
would be kept, and prepared him to expect all
that afterward followed.

164 WILLIAM THE CONQUEROR.

Harold's brother Tostig.   He brings intelligence of Harold's accession.

CHAPTER VIII.

THE PREPARATIONS.

THE messenger who brought William the tidings of Harold's accession to the throne was a man named Tostig, Harold's brother. Though he was Harold's brother, he was still his bitterest enemy. Brothers are seldom friends in families where there is a crown to be contended for. There were, of course, no public modes of communicating intelligence in those days, and Tostig had learned the facts of Edward's death and Harold's coronation through spies which he had stationed at certain points on the coast. He was himself, at that time, on the Continent. He rode with all speed to Rouen to communicate the news to William, eager to incite him to commence hostilities against his brother.

When Tostig arrived at Rouen, William was in a park which lay in the vicinity of the city, trying a new bow that had been recently made for him. William was a man of prodigious muscular strength, and they gave him the credit

WILLIAM RECEIVING TOSTIG'S TIDINGS.

of being able to use easily a bow which nobody else could bend. A part of this credit was doubtless due to the etiquette which, in royal palaces and grounds, leads all sensible courtiers to take good care never to succeed in attempts to excel the king. But, notwithstanding this consideration, there is no doubt that the duke really merited a great portion of the commendation that he received for his strength and dexterity in the use of the bow. It was a weapon in which he took great interest. A new one had been made for him, of great elasticity and strength, and he had gone out into his park, with his officers, to try its powers, when Tostig arrived. Tostig followed him to the place, and there advancing to his side, communicated the tidings to him privately.

William was greatly moved by the intelligence. His arrow dropped upon the ground. He gave the bow to an attendant. He stood for a time speechless, tying and untying the cordon of his cloak in his abstraction. Presently he began slowly to move away from the place, and to return toward the city. His attendants followed him in silence, wondering what the exciting tidings could be which had produced so sudden and powerful an effect.

William went into the castle hall, and walked to and fro a long time, thoughtful, and evidently agitated.   His attendants waited in silence, afraid to speak to him.   Rumors began
at length to circulate among them in respect to
the nature of the intelligence which had been
received.   At length a great officer of state,
named Fitzosborne, arrived at the castle.   As
he passed through the court-yard and gates, the
attendants and the people, knowing that he possessed in a great degree the confidence of his
sovereign, asked him what the tidings were that
had made such an impression.   " I know nothing certain about it," said he, " but I will soon
learn."   So saying, he advanced toward William, and accosted him by saying, " Why should
you conceal from us your news ?   It is reported in the city that the King of England is dead,
and that Harold has violated his oaths to you,
and has seized the kingdom.   Is that true ?"

William acknowledged that that was the intelligence by which he had been so vexed and
chagrined.   Fitzosborne urged the duke not to
allow such events to depress or dispirit him.
" As for the death of Edward," said he, " that
is an event past and sure, and can not be re-
called ; but Harold's usurpation and treachery

admits of a very easy remedy. You have the right to the throne, and you have the soldiers necessary to enforce that right. Undertake the enterprise boldly. You will be sure to succeed."

William revolved the subject in his mind for a few days, during which the exasperation and anger which the first receipt of the intelligence had produced upon him was succeeded by calm but indignant deliberation, in respect to the course which he should pursue. He concluded to call a great council of state, and to lay the case before them—not for the purpose of obtaining their advice, but to call their attention to the crisis in a formal and solemn manner, and to prepare them to act in concert in the subsequent measures to be pursued. The result of the deliberations of this council, guided, doubtless, by William's own designs, was, that the first step should be to send an embassy to Harold to demand of him the fulfillment of his promises.

The messenger was accordingly dispatched. He proceeded to London, and laid before Harold the communication with which he had been intrusted. This communication recounted the three promises which Harold had made, namely, to send his daughter to Normandy to be

married to one of William's generals ; to marry
William's daughter himself; and to maintain
William's claims to the English crown on the
death of Edward. He was to remind Harold,
also, of the solemnity with which he had bound
himself to fulfill these obligations, by oaths tak-
en in the presence of the most sacred relics of
the Church, and in the most public and deliberate manner.

Harold replied,

1. That as to sending over his daughter to be
married to one of William's generals, he could
not do it, for his daughter was dead. He pre-
sumed, he said, that William did not wish him
to send the corpse.

2. In respect to marrying William's daughter,
to whom he had been affianced in Normandy,
he was sorry to say that that was also out of
his power, as he could not take a foreign wife
without the consent of his people, which he was
confident would never be given ; besides, he
was already married, he said, to a Saxon lady
of his own dominions.

3. In regard to the kingdom : it did not depend upon him, he said, to decide who should
rule over England as Edward's successor, but
upon the will of Edward himself, and upon the

English people. The English barons and nobles had decided, with Edward's concurrence,
that he, Harold, was their legitimate and proper
sovereign, and that it was not for him to con-
trovert their will. However much he might be
disposed to comply with William's wishes, and
to keep his promise, it was plain that it was out
of his power, for in promising him the English
crown, he had promised what did not belong to
him to give.

4. As to his oaths, he said that, notwithstanding the secret presence of the sacred relics
under the cloth of gold, he considered them as
of no binding force upon his conscience, for he
was constrained to take them as the only means
of escaping from the duress in which he was
virtually held in Normandy. Promises, and
oaths even, when extorted by necessity, were
null and void.

The messenger returned to Normandy with
these replies, and William immediately began
to prepare for war.

His first measure was to call a council of his
most confidential friends and advisers, and to
lay the subject before them. They cordially
approved of the plan of an invasion of England,
and promised to co-operate in the accomplishment of it to the utmost of their power.

The next step was to call a general council of all the chieftains and nobles of the land, and also the *notables*, as they were called, or principal officers and municipal authorities of the *towns*. The main point of interest for the consideration of this assembly was, whether the country would submit to the necessary taxation for raising the necessary funds. William had ample power, as duke, to decide upon the invasion and to undertake it. He could also, without much difficulty, raise the necessary number of men; for every baron in his realm was bound, by the feudal conditions on which he held his land, to furnish his quota of men for any military enterprise in which his sovereign might see fit to engage. But for so distant and vast an undertaking as this, William needed a much larger supply of *funds* than were usually required in the wars of those days. For raising such large supplies, the political institutions of the Middle Ages had not made any adequate provision. Governments then had no power of taxation, like that so freely exercised in modern times; and even now, taxes in France and England take the form of *grants* from the people to the kings. And as to the contrivance, so exceedingly ingenious, by which

inexhaustible resources are opened to governments at the present day—that is, the plan of
borrowing the money, and leaving posterity to
pay or repudiate the debt, as they please, no
minister of finance had, in William's day, been
brilliant enough to discover it. Thus each
ruler had to rely, then, mainly on the rents and
income from his own lands, and other private
resources, for the comparatively small amount
of money that he needed in his brief campaigns.
But now William perceived that ships must be
built and equipped, and great stores of provisions
accumulated, and arms and munitions of war
provided, all which would require a considerable outlay; and how was this money to be obtained?

The general assembly which he convened
were greatly distracted by the discussion of the
question. The quiet and peaceful citizens who
inhabited the towns, the artisans and trades-
men, who wished for nothing but to be allowed
to go on in their industrial pursuits in peace,
were opposed to the whole project. They
thought it unreasonable and absurd that they
should be required to contribute from their earn-
ings to enable their lord and master to go off on
so distant and desperate an undertaking, from

which, even if successful, they could derive no
benefit whatever.   Many of the barons, too,
were opposed to the scheme.   They thought it
very likely to end in disaster and defeat; and
they denied that their feudal obligation to furnish men for their sovereign's wars was binding
to the extent of requiring them to go out of the
country, and beyond the sea, to prosecute his
claims to the throne of another kingdom.

Others, on the other hand, among the members of William's assembly, were strongly disposed to favor the plan.   They were more ardent or more courageous than the rest, or perhaps their position and circumstances were
such that they had more to hope from the success of the enterprise than they, or less to fear
from its failure.   Thus there was great diversity
of opinion; and as the parliamentary system
of rules, by which a body of turbulent men, in
modern times, are kept in some semblance of
organization and order during a debate, had not
then been developed, the meeting of these Norman deliberators was, for a time, a scene of up-
roar and confusion.   The members gathered in
groups, each speaker getting around him as
many as he could obtain to listen to his ha-
rangue; the more quiet and passive portion of

the assembly moving to and fro, from group to
group, as they were attracted by the earnest-
ness and eloquence of the different speakers, or
by their approval of the sentiments which they
heard them expressing. The scene, in fact,
was like that presented in exciting times by a
political caucus in America, before it is called
to order by the chairman.

Fitzosborne, the confidential friend and coun-
selor, who has already been mentioned as the
one who ventured to accost the duke at the
time when the tidings of Edward's death and
of Harold's accession first reached him, now
seeing that any thing like definite and harmo-
nious action on the part of this tumultuous assembly was out of the question, went to the
duke, and proposed to him to give up the assembly as such, and make the best terms and
arrangements that he could with the constitu-
ent elements of it, individually and severally.
He would himself, he said, furnish forty ships,
manned, equipped, and provisioned; and he recommended to the duke to call each of the others
into his presence, and ask them what they were
individually willing to do. The duke .adopted
this plan, and it was wonderfully successful.
Those who were first invited made large offers,

and their offers were immediately registered in
form by the proper officers.   Each one who followed was emulous of the example of those who
had preceded him, and desirous of evincing as
much zeal and generosity as they.   Then, besides, the duke received these vassals with so
much condescension and urbanity, and treated
them with so much consideration and respect,
as greatly to flatter their vanity, and raise them
in their own estimation, by exalting their ideas
of the importance of the services which they
could render in carrying so vast an enterprise
to a successful result.   In a word, the tide turned like a flood in favor of granting liberal supplies.   The nobles and knights promised freely
men, money, ships, arms, provisions — every
thing, in short, that was required; and when
the work of receiving and registering the offers
was completed, and the officers summed up the
aggregate amount, William found, to his extreme satisfaction, that his wants were abun-
dantly supplied.

There was another very important point,
which William adopted immediate measures to
secure, and that was obtaining the *Pope's* approval of his intended expedition.   The moral
influence of having the Roman pontiff on his

side, would, he knew, be of incalculable advantage to him. He sent an embassage, accordingly, to Rome, to lay the whole subject before his holiness, and to pray that the pope would declare that he was justly entitled to the English crown, and authorize him to proceed and take possession of it by force of arms. Lanfranc was the messenger whom he employed—the same Lanfranc who had been so successful, some years before, in the negotiations at Rome connected with the confirmation of William and Matilda's marriage.

Lanfranc was equally successful now. The pope, after examining William's claims, pronounced them valid. He decided that William was entitled to the rank and honors of King of England. He caused a formal diploma to be made out to this effect. The diploma was elegantly executed, signed with the cross, according to the pontifical custom, and sealed with a round leaden seal.*

It was, in fact, very natural that the Roman authorities should take a favorable view of William's enterprise, and feel an interest in its suc.

---

* The Latin name for such a seal was *bulla*. It is on account of this sort of seal, which is customarily affixed to them, that papal edicts have received the name of *bulls*.

28—12

cess, as it was undoubtedly for the interest of
the Church that William, rather than Harold,
should reign over England, as the accession of
William would bring the English realm far
more fully under the influence of the Roman
Church.   William had always been very submissive to the pontifical authority, as was shown
in his conduct in respect to the question of his
marriage.   He himself, and also Matilda his
wife, had always taken a warm interest in the
welfare and prosperity of the abbeys, the monasteries, the churches, and the other religious
establishments of the times.   Then the very circumstance that he sent his embassador to Rome
to submit his claims to the pontiff's adjudica-
tion, while Harold did not do so, indicated a
greater deference for the authority of the Church,
and made it probable that he would be a far
more obedient and submissive son of the Church,
in his manner of ruling his realm, if he should
succeed in gaining possession of it, than Harold his rival.   The pope and his counselors at
Rome thought it proper to take all these things
into the account in deciding between William
and Harold, as they honestly believed, without
doubt, that it was their first and highest duty to
exalt and aggrandize, by every possible means,

A.D. 1066.] THE PREPARATIONS. 179

The banner and the ring.   Excitement produced by their reception.

the spiritual authority of the sacred institution over which they were called to preside.

The pope and his cardinals, accordingly, espoused William's cause very warmly. In addition to the diploma which gave William formal authority to take possession of the English crown, the pope sent him a banner and a ring. The banner was of costly and elegant workmanship; its value, however, did not consist in its elegance or its cost, but in a solemn benediction which his holiness pronounced over it, by which it was rendered sacred and inviolable. The banner, thus blessed, was forwarded to William by Lanfranc with great care.

It was accompanied by the ring. The ring was of gold, and it contained a diamond of great value. The gold and the diamond both, however, served only as settings to preserve and honor something of far greater value than they. This choice treasure was a hair from the head of the Apostle Peter! a sacred relic of miraculous virtue and of inestimable value.

When the edict with its leaden seal, and the banner and the ring arrived in Normandy, they produced a great and universal excitement. To have bestowed upon the enterprise thus emphatically the solemn sanction of the great spiritual

head of the Church, to whom the great mass of
the people looked up with an awe and a rever-
ence almost divine, was to seal indissolubly the
rightfulness of the enterprise, and to insure its
success.   There was thenceforward no difficulty
in procuring men or means.   Every body was
eager to share in the glory, and to obtain the
rewards, of an enterprise thus commended by
an authority duly commissioned to express, in
all such cases, the judgment of Heaven.

Finding that the current was thus fairly setting in his favor, William sent proclamations
into all the countries surrounding Normandy,
inviting knights, and soldiers, and adventurers
of every degree to join him in his projected enterprise.   These proclamations awakened universal attention.   Great numbers of adventurous men determined to enter William's service.
Horses, arms, and accoutrements were every
where in great demand.   The invasion of England and the question of joining it were the
universal topics of conversation.   The roads
were covered with knights and soldiers, some
on horseback and alone, others in bands, large
or small, all proceeding to Normandy to tender
their services.   William received them all, and
made liberal promises to bestow rewards and

honors upon them in England, in the event of his success. To some he offered pay in money; to others, booty; to others, office and power. Every one had his price. Even the priests and dignitaries of the Church shared the general enthusiasm. One of them furnished a ship and twenty armed men, under an agreement to be appointed bishop of a certain valuable English diocese when William should be established on his throne.

While all these movements were going on in the interior of the country, all the sea-ports and towns along the coast of Normandy presented a very busy scene of naval preparation. Naval architects were employed in great numbers in building and fitting out vessels. Some were constructed and furnished for the transportation of men, others for conveying provisions and munitions of war; and lighters and boats were built for ascending the rivers, and for aiding in landing troops upon shelving shores. Smiths and armorers were occupied incessantly in manufacturing spears, and swords, and coats of mail; while vast numbers of laboring men and beasts of burden were employed in conveying arms and materials to and from the manufactories to the ships, and from one point of embarkation to another.

As soon as William had put all these busy
agencies thus in successful operation, he considered that there was one more point which it
was necessary for him to secure before finally
embarking, and that was the co-operation and
aid of the French king, whose name at this time
was Philip.   In his character of Duke of Normandy the King of France was his liege lord,
and he was bound to act, in some degree, under
an acknowledgment of his superior authority.
In his new capacity, that is, as King of England, or, rather, as heir to the English kingdom,
he was, of course, wholly independent of Philip,
and, consequently, not bound by any feudal obligation to look to him at all.   He thought it
most prudent, however, to attempt, at least, to
conciliate Philip's favor, and, accordingly, leaving his officers and his workmen to go on with
the work of organizing his army and of building and equipping the fleet, he set off, himself,
on an expedition to the court of the French
king.   He thought it safer to undertake this
delicate mission himself, rather than to intrust
it to an embassador or deputy.

He found Philip at his palace of St. Ger-
main's, which was situated at a short distance
from Paris.   The duke assumed, in his inter-

view with the king, a very respectful and def-
erential air and manner. Philip was a very
young man, though haughty and vain. William was very much his superior, not only in
age and experience, but in talents and character, and in personal renown. Still, he approached the monarch with all the respectful observ-
ance due from a vassal to his sovereign, made
known his plans, and asked for Philip's appro-
bation and aid. He was willing, he said, in
case that aid was afforded him, to hold his kingdom of England, as he had done the duchy
of Normandy, as a dependency of the French
crown.

Philip seemed not at all disposed to look upon
the project with favor. He asked William who
was going to take care of his duchy while he
was running off after a kingdom. William replied, at first, that that was a subject which he
did not think his neighbors need concern themselves about. Then thinking, on reflection,
that a more respectful answer would be more
politic, under the circumstances of the case, he
added, that he was providentially blessed with
a prudent wife and loving subjects, and that he
thought he might safely leave his domestic affairs in their hands until he should return.

Philip still opposed the plan. It was Quixotic, he said, and dangerous. He strongly advised William to abandon the scheme, and be content with his present possessions. Such desperate schemes of ambition as those he was contemplating would only involve him in ruin.

Before absolutely deciding the case, however, Philip called a council of his great nobles and officers of state, and laid William's proposals before them. The result of their deliberations was to confirm Philip in his first decision. They said that the rendering to William the aid which he desired would involve great expense, and be attended with great danger; and as to William's promises to hold England as a vassal of the King of France, they had no faith in the performance of them. It had been very difficult, they said, for many years, for the kings of France to maintain any effectual authority over the dukes of Normandy, and when once master of so distant and powerful a realm as England, all control over them would be sundered forever.

Philip then gave William his final answer in accordance with these counsels. The answer was received, on William's part, with strong feelings of disappointment and displeasure. Philip conducted the duke to his retinue when the hour of departure arrived, in order to soothe, as far as possible, his irritated feelings, by dismissing him from his court with marks of his honorable consideration and regard. William, however, was not in a mood to be pleased. He told Philip, on taking leave of him, that he was losing the most powerful vassal that any lord sovereign ever had, by the course which he had decided to pursue. " I would have held the whole realm of England as a part of your dominions, acknowledging you as sovereign over all, if you had consented to render me your aid, but I will not do it since you refuse. I shall feel bound to repay only those who assist me."

William returned to Normandy, where all the preparations for the expedition had been going on with great vigor during his absence, and proceeded to make arrangements for the last great measure which it was necessary to take previous to his departure; that was, the regular constitution of a government to rule in Normandy while he should be gone. He determined to leave the supreme power in the hands of his wife Matilda, appointing, at the same time, a number of civil and military officers as a council of regency, who were to assist her in her deliberations by giving her informa-

tion and advice, and to manage, under her direction, the different departments of the government.   Her title was "Duchess Regent," and
she was installed into her office in a public and
solemn manner, at a great assembly of the estates of the realm.   At the close of the ceremonies, after William had given Matilda his
charge, he closed his address by adding, "And
do not let us fail to enjoy the benefit of your
prayers, and those of all the ladies of your court,
that the blessing of God may attend us, and
secure the success of our expedition."

We are not necessarily to suppose, as we
might at first be strongly inclined to do, that
there was any special hypocrisy and pretense
in William's thus professing to rely on the protection of Heaven in the personal and political
dangers which he was about to incur.   It is
probable that he honestly believed that the inheritance of the English crown was his right,
and, that being the case, that a vigorous and
manly effort to enforce his right was a solemn
duty.   In the present age of the world, now
that there are so many countries in which intelligence, industry, and love of order are so ex-
tensively diffused that the mass of the community are capable of organizing and administering

a government themselves, republicans are apt
to look upon hereditary sovereigns as despots,
ruling only for the purpose of promoting their
own aggrandizement, and the ends of an un-
holy and selfish ambition. That there have
been a great many such despots no one can
deny; but then, on the other hand, there have
been many others who have acted, in a greater
or less degree, under the influence of principles
of duty in their political career. They have
honestly believed that the vast power with
which, in coming forward into life, they have
found themselves invested, without, in most
cases, any agency of their own, was a trust imposed upon them by divine Providence, which
could not innocently be laid aside; that on them
devolved the protection of the communities over
which they ruled from external hostility, and
the preservation of peace and order within, and
the promotion of the general industry and welfare, as an imperious and solemn duty; and
they have devoted their lives to the performance
of this duty, with the usual mixture, it is true,
of ambition and selfishness, but still, after all,
with as much conscientiousness and honesty as
the mass of men in the humbler walks of life
evince in performing theirs. William of Nor-

mandy appears to have been one of this latter
class; and in obeying the dictates of his ambition in seeking to gain possession of the English
crown, he no doubt considered himself as fulfilling the obligations of duty too.

However this may be, he went on with his
preparations in the most vigorous and prosperous manner.   The whole country were enthusi-
astic in the cause; and their belief that the
enterprise about to be undertaken had unques-
tionably secured the favor of Heaven, was confirmed by an extraordinary phenomenon which
occurred just before the armament was ready
to set sail.   A comet appeared in the sky,
which, as close observers declared, had a double
tail.   It was universally agreed that this por-
tended that England and Normandy were about
to be combined, and to form a double kingdom,
which should exhibit to all mankind a wonder-
ful spectacle of splendor.

CHAPTER IX.

CROSSING THE CHANNEL.

THE place for the final assembling of the
fleet which was to convey the expedition
across the Channel was the mouth of a small
river called the Dive, which will be seen upon
the following map, flowing from the neighborhood of the castle of Falaise northward into the

NORMANDY.

sea. The grand gathering took place in the be-
ginning of the month of September, in the year
1066. This date, which marks the era of the
Norman Conquest, is one of the dates which
students of history fix indelibly in the memory.

The gathering of the fleet in the estuary of
the Dive, and the assembling of the troops on
the beach along its shores, formed a very grand
and imposing spectacle. The fleets of galleys,
ships, boats, and barges covering the surface of
the water—the long lines of tents under the
cliffs on the land—the horsemen, splendidly
mounted, and glittering with steel—the groups
of soldiers, all busily engaged in transporting
provisions and stores to and fro, or making the
preliminary arrangements for the embarkation
—the thousands of spectators who came and
went incessantly, and the duke himself, gorgeously dressed, and mounted on his war-horse,
with the guards and officers that attended him
—these, and the various other elements of martial parade and display usually witnessed on
such occasions, conspired to produce a very gay
and brilliant, as well as magnificent scene.

Of course, the assembling of so large a force
of men and of vessels, and the various preparations for the embarkation, consumed some time,

and when at length all was ready—which was
early in September—the equinoctial gales came
on, and it was found impossible to leave the
port. There was, in fact, a continuance of
heavy winds and seas, and stormy skies, for several weeks. Short intervals, from time to time,
occurred, when the clouds would break away,
and the sun appear; but these intervals did not
liberate the fleet from its confinement, for they
were not long enough in duration to allow the
sea to go down. The surf continued to come
rolling and thundering in upon the shore, and
over the sand-bars at the mouth of the river,
making destruction the almost inevitable destiny of any ship which should undertake to brave
its fury. The state of the skies gradually rob-
bed the scene of the gay and brilliant colors
which first it wore. The vessels furled their
sails, and drew in their banners, and rode at
anchor, presenting their heads doggedly to the
storm. The men on the shore sought shelter
in their tents. The spectators retired to their
homes, while the duke and his officers watched
the scudding clouds in the sky, day after day,
with great and increasing anxiety.

In fact, William had very serious cause for
apprehension in respect to the effect which this

long-continued storm was to have on the success of his enterprise. The delay was a very
serious consideration in itself, for the winter
would soon be drawing near. In one month
more it would seem to be out of the question
for such a vast armament to cross the Channel
at all. Then, when men are embarking in
such dark and hazardous undertakings as that
in which William was now engaged, their spirits and their energy rise and sink in great fluc-
tuations, under the influence of very slight and
inadequate causes ; and nothing has greater influence over them at such times than the aspect
of the skies. William found that the ardor and
enthusiasm of his army were fast disappearing
under the effects of chilling winds and driving
rain. The feelings of discontent and depression
which the frowning expression of the heavens
awakened in their minds, were deepened and
spread by the influence of sympathy. The
men had nothing to do, during the long and
dreary hours of the day, but to anticipate hardships and dangers, and to entertain one another,
as they watched the clouds driving along the
cliffs, and the rolling of the surges in the offing,
with anticipations of shipwrecks, battles, and
defeats, and all the other gloomy forebodings

which haunt the imagination of a discouraged
and discontented soldier.

Nor were these ideas of wrecks and destruction wholly imaginary. Although the body of
the fleet remained in the river, where it was
sheltered from the winds, yet there were many
cases of single ships that were from time to
time exposed to them. These were detached
vessels coming in late to the rendezvous, or
small squadrons sent out to some neighboring
port under some necessity connected with the
preparations, or strong galleys, whose com-
manders, more bold than the rest, were willing,
in cases *not* of absolute necessity, to brave the
danger. Many of these vessels were wrecked.
The fragments of them, with the bodies of the
drowned mariners, were driven to the shore.
The ghastly spectacles presented by these dead
bodies, swollen and mangled, and half buried
in the sand, as if the sea had been endeavoring
to hide the mischief it had done, shocked and
terrified the spectators who saw them. William gave orders to have all these bodies gathered up and interred secretly, as fast as they
were found; still, exaggerated rumors of the
number and magnitude of these disasters were
circulated in the camp, and the discontent and

28—13

apprehensions grew every day more and more alarming.

William resolved that he must put to sea at the very first possible opportunity. The favorable occasion was not long wanting. The wind changed. The storm appeared to cease. A breeze sprang up from the south, which headed back the surges from the French shore. William gave orders to embark. The tents were struck. The baggage of the soldiers was sent on board the transport vessels. The men themselves, crowded into great flat-bottomed boats, passed in masses to the ships from the shore. The spectators reappeared, and covered the cliffs and promontories near, to witness the final scene. The sails were hoisted, and the vast armament moved out upon the sea.

The appearance of a favorable change in the weather proved fallacious after all, for the clouds and storm returned, and after being driven, in apprehension and danger, about a hundred miles to the northeast along the coast, the fleet was compelled to seek refuge again in a harbor. The port which received them was St. Valery, near Dieppe. The duke was greatly disappointed at being obliged thus again to take the land. Still, the attempt to advance had not been a labor wholly lost; for as the French coast here trends to the northward, they had been gradually narrowing the channel as they proceeded, and were, in fact, so far on the way toward the English shores. Then there were, besides, some reasons for touching here, before the final departure, to receive some last re-enforcements and supplies. William had also one more opportunity of communicating with his capital and with Matilda.

These delays, disastrous as they seemed to be, and ominous of evil, were nevertheless attended with one good effect, of which, however, William at the time was not aware. They led Harold, in England, to imagine that the enterprise was abandoned, and so put him off his guard. There were in those days, as has already been remarked, no regular and public modes of intercommunication, by which intelligence of important movements and events was spread every where, as now, with promptness and certainty. Governments were obliged, accordingly, to rely for information, in respect to what their enemies were doing, on rumors, or on the reports of spies. Rumors had gone to England in August that William was meditating an invasion, and Harold had made some extensive preparations to meet and oppose him; but, finding that he did not come—that week after week of September passed away, and no signs of an enemy appeared, and gaining no certain information of the causes of the delay, he concluded that the enterprise was abandoned, or else, perhaps, postponed to the ensuing spring. Accordingly, as the winter was coming on, he deemed it best to commence his preparations for sending his troops to their winter quarters. He disbanded some of them, and sent others away, distributing them in various castles and fortified towns, where they would be sheltered from the rigors of the season, and saved from the exposure and hardships of the camp, and yet, at the same time, remain within reach of a summons in case of any sudden emergency which might call for them. They were soon summoned, though not, in the first instance, to meet Harold, as will presently appear.

While adopting these measures, however, which he thought the comfort and safety of his army required, Harold did not relax his vigilance in watching, as well as he could, the designs and movements of his enemy. He kept his secret agents on the southern coast, ordering

them to observe closely every thing that trans-
pired, and to gather and send to him every item
of intelligence which should find its way by any
means across the Channel. Of course, William would do all in his power to intercept and
cut off all communication, and he was, at this
time, very much aided in these efforts by the
prevalence of the storms, which made it almost
impossible for the fishing and trading vessels
of the coast to venture out to sea, or attempt
to cross the Channel. The agents of Harold,
therefore, on the southern coast of England,
found that they could obtain but very little information.

At length the king, unwilling to remain any
longer so entirely in the dark, resolved on sending some messengers across the sea into Normandy itself, to learn positively what the true
state of the case might be. Messengers going
thus secretly into the enemy's territory, or into
the enemy's camp, become, by so doing, in martial law, *spies*, and incur, if they are taken, the
penalty of death. The undertaking, therefore,
is extremely hazardous; and as the death which
is inflicted in cases of detection is an ignominious one — spies being hung, not shot — most
men are very averse to encountering the dan-

13

ger. Still, desperate characters are always to
be found in camps and armies, who are ready
to undertake it on being promised very extraordinary pay.

Harold's spies contrived to make their way
across the Channel, probably at some point far
to the east of Normandy, where the passage is
narrow. They then came along the shore, disguised as peasants of the country, and they arrived at St. Valery while William's fleets were
there. Here they began to make their observa-
tions, scrutinizing every thing with close attention and care, and yet studiously endeavoring
to conceal their interest in what they saw.
Notwithstanding all their vigilance, however,
they were discovered, proved to be spies, and
taken before William to receive their sentence.

Instead of condemning them to death, which
they undoubtedly supposed would be their inevitable fate, William ordered them to be set at
liberty. " Go back," said he, " to King Harold, and tell him he might have saved himself
the expense of sending spies into Normandy to
learn what I am preparing for him. He will
soon know by other means—much sooner, in
fact, than he imagines. Go and tell him from
me that he may put himself, if he pleases, in

the safest place he can find in all his dominions, and if he does not find my hand upon him before the year is out, he never need fear me again as long as he lives."

Nor was this expression of confidence in the success of the measures which he was taking a mere empty boast. William knew the power of Harold, and he knew his own. The enterprise in which he had embarked was not a rash adventure. It was a cool, deliberate, well-considered plan. It appeared doubtful and dangerous in the eyes of mankind, for to mere superficial observers it seemed simply an aggressive war waged by a duke of Normandy, the ruler of a comparatively small and insignificant province, against a king of England, the monarch of one of the greatest and most powerful realms in the world. William, on the other hand, regarded it as an effort on the part of the rightful heir to a throne to dispossess a usurper. He felt confident of having the sympathy and co-operation of a great part of the community, even in England, the moment he could show them that he was able to maintain his rights; and that he could show them that, by a very decisive demonstration, was evident, visibly, before him, in the vast fleet which was riding at

anchor in the harbor, and in the long lines of
tents, filled with soldiery, which covered the
land.

On one occasion, when some of his officers
were expressing apprehensions of Harold's power, and their fears in respect to their being able
successfully to cope with it, William replied,
that the more formidable Harold's power should
prove to be, the better he should be pleased, as
the glory would be all the greater for them in
having overcome it. " I have no objection,"
said he, " that you should entertain exalted
ideas of his strength, though I wonder a little
that you do not better appreciate our own. I
need be under no concern lest he, at such a distance, should learn too much, by his spies, about
the force which I am bringing against him,
when you, who are so near me, seem to know
so little about it. But do not give yourselves
any concern. Trust to the justice of your
cause and to my foresight. Perform your parts
like men, and you will find that the result
which I feel sure of, and you hope for, will cer-
tainly be attained."

The storm at length entirely cleared away,
and the army and the fleet commenced their
preparations for the final departure. In the

midst of this closing scene, the attention of all
the vast crowds assembled on board the ships
and on the shores was one morning attracted
by a beautiful ship which came sailing into the
harbor.   It proved to be a large and splendid
vessel which the Duchess Matilda had built, at
her own expense, and was now bringing in, to
offer to her husband as her parting gift.   She
was herself on board, with her officers and attendants, having come to witness her husband's
departure, and to bid him farewell.   Her arrival, of course, under such circumstances, produced universal excitement and enthusiasm.
The ships in harbor and the shores resounded
with acclamations as the new arrival came gal-
lantly in.

Matilda's vessel was finely built and splendidly decorated.   The sails were of different
colors, which gave it a very gay appearance.
Upon them were painted, in various places, the
three lions, which was the device of the Norman ensign.   At the bows of the ship was an
effigy, or figure-head, representing William and
Matilda's second son shooting with a bow.   This
was the accomplishment which, of all others,
his father took most interest in seeing his little
son acquire.   The arrow was drawn nearly to

its head, indicating great strength in the little
arms which were guiding it, and it was just
ready to fly. The name of this vessel was the
Mira. William made it his flag ship. He hoisted upon its mast head the consecrated banner
which had been sent to him from Rome, and
went on board accompanied by his officers and
guards, and with great ceremony and parade.

At length the squadron was ready to put to
sea. At a given signal the sails were hoisted,
and the whole fleet began to move slowly out
of the harbor. There were four hundred ships
of large size, if we may believe the chronicles
of the times, and more than a thousand trans-
ports. The decks of all these vessels were covered with men ; banners were streaming from
every mast and spar ; and every salient point
of the shore was crowded with spectators. The
sea was calm, the air serene, and the mighty
cloud of canvas which whitened the surface of
the water moved slowly on over the gentle swell
of the waves, forming a spectacle which, as a
picture merely for the eye, was magnificent and
grand, and, when regarded in connection with
the vast results to the human race which were
to flow from the success of the enterprise, must
have been considered sublime.

The splendidly decorated ship which Matilda
had presented to her husband proved itself, on
trial, to be something more than a mere toy.
It led the van at the commencement, of course ;
and as all eyes watched its progress, it soon became evident that it was slowly gaining upon
the rest of the squadron, so as continually to
increase its distance from those that were following it. William, pleased with the success
of its performance, ordered the sailing master
to keep on, without regard to those who were
behind ; and thus it happened that, when night
came on, the fleet was at very considerable
distance in rear of the flag ship. Of course,
under these circumstances, the fleet disappeared from sight when the sun went down, but all
expected that it would come into view again in
the morning. When the morning came, however, to the surprise and disappointment of every one on board the flag ship, no signs of the
fleet were to be seen. The seamen, and the
officers on the deck, gazed long and intently
into the southern horizon as the increasing light
of the morning brought it gradually into view,
but there was not a speck to break its smooth
and even line.

They felt anxious and uneasy, but William

seemed to experience no concern. He ordered the sails to be furled, and then sent a man to the mast head to look out there. Nothing was to be seen. William, still apparently unconcerned, ordered breakfast to be prepared in a very sumptuous manner, loading the tables with wine and other delicacies, that the minds of all on board might be cheered by the exhilarating influence of a feast. At length the lookout was sent to the mast head again. "What do you see now?" said William. "I see," said the man, gazing very intently all the while toward the south, "four *very small specks* just in the horizon." The intense interest which this announcement awakened on the deck was soon at the same time *heightened* and *relieved* by the cry, "I can see more and more—they are the ships—yes, the whole squadron is coming into view."

The advancing fleet soon came up with the Mira, when the latter spread her sails again, and all moved slowly on together toward the coast of England.

The ships had directed their course so much to the eastward, that when they made the land they were not very far from the Straits of Dover. As they drew near to the English shore,

they watched very narrowly for the appearance
of Harold's cruisers, which they naturally expected would have been stationed at various
points, to guard the coast; but none were to be
seen. There had been such cruisers, and there
still were such off the other harbors; but it
happened, very fortunately for William, that
those which had been stationed to guard this
part of the island had been withdrawn a few
days before, on account of their provisions being exhausted. Thus, when William's fleet
arrived, there was no enemy to oppose their
landing. There was a large and open bay, called the Bay of Pevensey, which lay smiling before them, extending its arms as if inviting
them in. The fleet advanced to within the
proper distance from the land, and there the
seamen cast their anchors, and all began to
prepare for the work of disembarkation.

A strong body of soldiery is of course landed
first on such occasions. In this instance the
archers, William's favorite corps, were selected
to take the lead. William accompanied them.
In his eagerness to get to the shore, as he leaped from the boat, his foot slipped, and he fell.
The officers and men around him would have
considered this an evil omen; but he had pres-

ence of mind enough to extend his arms and grasp the ground, pretending that his prostration was designed, and saying at the same time, " Thus I seize this land; from this moment it is mine." As he arose, one of his officers ran to a neighboring hut which stood near by upon the shore, and breaking off a little of the thatch, carried it to William, and, putting it into his hand, said that he thus gave him *seizin* of his new possessions. This was a customary form, in those times, of putting a new owner into possession of lands which he had purchased or acquired in any other way. The new proprietor would repair to the ground, where the party whose province it was to deliver the property would detach something from it, such as a piece of turf from a bank, or a little of the thatch from a cottage, and offering it to him, would say, " Thus I deliver thee *seizin*," that is, *possession*, "of this land." This ceremony was necessary to complete the conveyance of the estate.

The soldiers, as soon as they were landed, began immediately to form an encampment, and to make such military arrangements as were necessary to guard against an attack, or the sudden appearance of an enemy. While this was going on, the boats continued to pass to and fro, accomplishing, as fast as possible, the work of disembarkation. In addition to those regularly attached to the army, there was a vast company of workmen of all kinds, engineers, pioneers, carpenters, masons, and laborers, to be landed; and there were three towers, or rather forts, built of timber, which had been framed and fashioned in Normandy, ready to be put up on arriving: these had now to be landed, piece by piece, on the strand. These forts were to be erected as soon as the army should have chosen a position for a permanent encampment, and were intended as a means of protection for the provisions and stores. The circumstance shows that the plan of transporting buildings ready made, across the seas, has not been invented anew by our emigrants to California.

While these operations were going on, William dispatched small squadrons of horse as reconnoitering parties, to explore the country around, to see if there were any indications that Harold was near. These parties returned, one after another, after having gone some miles into the country in all directions, and reported that there were no signs of an enemy to

be seen.   Things were now getting settled, too,
in the camp, and William gave directions that
the army should kindle their camp fires for the
night, and prepare and eat their suppers.   His
own supper, or dinner, as perhaps it might be
called, was also served, which he partook, with
his officers, in his own tent.   His mind was in
a state of great contentment and satisfaction at
the successful accomplishment of the landing,
and at finding himself thus safely established,
at the head of a vast force, within the realm of
England.

Every circumstance of the transit had been
favorable excepting one, and that was, that two
of the ships belonging to the fleet were missing.
William inquired at supper if any tidings of
them had been received.   They told him, in reply, that the missing vessels had been heard
from; they had, in some way or other, been
run upon the rocks and lost.   There was a
certain astrologer, who had made a great parade,
before the expedition left Normandy, of predict-
ing its result.   He had found, by consulting the
stars, that William would be successful, and
would meet with no opposition from Harold.
This astrologer had been on board one of the
missing ships, and was drowned.   William re-

marked, on receiving this information, "What an idiot a man must be, to think that he can predict, by means of the stars, the future fate of others, when it is so plain that he can not foresee his own!"

It is said that William's dinner on this occasion was served on a large stone instead of a table. The stone still remains on the spot, and is called "the Conqueror's Stone" to this day.

The next day after the landing, the army was put in motion, and advanced along the coast toward the eastward. There was no armed enemy to contend against them there or to oppose their march; the people of the country, through which the army moved, far from attempting to resist them, were filled with terror and dismay. This terror was heightened, in fact, by some excesses of which some parties of the soldiers were guilty. The inhabitants of the hamlets and villages, overwhelmed with consternation at the sudden descent upon their shores of such a vast horde of wild and desperate foreigners, fled in all directions. Some made their escape into the interior; others, taking with them the helpless members of their households, and such valuables as they could carry, sought refuge in monasteries and churches,

28—14

supposing that such sanctuaries as those, not even soldiers, unless they were pagans, would dare to violate. Others, still, attempted to conceal themselves in thickets and fens till the vast throng which was sweeping onward like a tornado should have passed. Though William afterward always evinced a decided disposition to protect the peaceful inhabitants of the country from all aggressions on the part of his troops, he had no time to attend to that subject now. He was intent on pressing forward to a place of safety.

William reached at length a position which seemed to him suitable for a permanent encampment. It was an elevated land, near the sea. To the westward of it was a valley formed by a sort of recess opened in the range of chalky cliffs which here form the shore of England. In the bottom of this valley, down upon the beach, was a small town, then of no great consequence or power, but whose name, which was Hastings, has since been immortalized by the battle which was fought in its vicinity a few days after William's arrival. The position which William selected for his encampment was on high land in the vicinity of the town. The lines of the encampment were marked out, and the forts or castles which had been brought from Normandy were set up within the inclosures. Vast multitudes of laborers were soon at work, throwing up embankments, and building redoubts and bastions, while others were transporting the arms, the provisions, and the munitions of war, and storing them in security within the lines. The encampment was soon completed, and the long line of tents were set up in streets and squares within it. By the time, however, that the work was done, some of William's agents and spies came into camp from the north, saying that in four days Harold would be upon him at the head of a hundred thousand men.

CHAPTER X.

THE BATTLE OF HASTINGS.

THE reader will doubtless recollect that the
tidings which William first received of the
accession of King Harold were brought to him
by Tostig, Harold's brother, on the day when
he was trying his bow and arrows in the park
at Rouen. Tostig was his brother's most inveterate foe.   He had been, during the reign of
Edward, a great chieftain, ruling over the north
of England. The city of York was then his
capital. He had been expelled from these his
dominions, and had quarreled with his brother
Harold in respect to his right to be restored to
them.   In the course of this quarrel he was
driven from the country altogether, and went
to the Continent, burning with rage and resentment against his brother ; and when he came
to inform William of Harold's usurpation, his
object was not merely to arouse *William* to action—he wished to act himself.   He told William that he himself had more influence in England still than his brother, and that if William

would supply him with a small fleet and a mod-
erate number of men, he would make a descent
upon the coast and show what he could do.

William acceded to his proposal, and furnished him with the force which he required, and
Tostig set sail. William had not, apparently,
much confidence in the power of Tostig to produce any great effect, but his efforts, he thought,
might cause some alarm in England, and occasion sudden and fatiguing marches to the troops,
and thus distract and weaken King Harold's
forces. William would not, therefore, accompany Tostig himself, but, dismissing him with
such force as he could readily raise on so sudden a call, he remained himself in Normandy,
and commenced in earnest his own grand preparations, as is described in the last chapter.

Tostig did not think it prudent to attempt a
landing on English shores until he had obtained some accession to the force which William
had given him. He accordingly passed through
the Straits of Dover, and then turning northward, he sailed along the eastern shores of the
German Ocean in search of allies. He came,
at length, to Norway. He entered into negotiations there with the Norwegian king, whose
name, too, was Harold. This northern Harold

14

was a wild and adventurous soldier and sailor,
a sort of sea king, who had spent a considerable portion of his life in marauding excursions
upon the seas. He readily entered into Tostig's views. An arrangement was soon concluded, and Tostig set sail again to cross the
German Ocean toward the British shores, while
Harold promised to collect and equip his own
fleet as soon as possible, and follow him. All
this took place early in September ; so that, at
the same time that William's threatened invasion was gathering strength and menacing Harold's southern frontier, a cloud equally dark and
gloomy, and quite as threatening in its aspect,
was rising and swelling in the north ; while
King Harold himself, though full of vague uneasiness and alarm, could gain no certain information in respect to either of these dangers.

The Norwegian fleet assembled at the port
appointed for the rendezvous of it, but, as the
season was advanced and the weather stormy,
the soldiers there, like William's soldiers on the
coast of France, were afraid to put to sea. Some
of them had dreams which they considered as
bad omens ; and so much superstitious importance was attached to such ideas in those times

that these dreams were gravely recorded by the writers of the ancient chronicles, and have come down to us as part of the regular and sober history of the times. One soldier dreamed that the expedition had sailed and landed on the English coast, and that there the English army came out to meet them. Before the front of the army rode a woman of gigantic stature, mounted on a wolf. The wolf had in his jaws a human body, dripping with blood, which he was engaged in devouring as he came along. The woman gave the wolf another victim after he had devoured the first.

Another of these ominous dreams was the following: Just as the fleet was about setting sail, the dreamer saw a crowd of ravenous vultures and birds of prey come and alight every where upon the sails and rigging of the ships, as if they were going to accompany the expedition. Upon the summit of a rock near the shore there sat the figure of a female, with a stern and ferocious countenance, and a drawn sword in her hand. She was busy counting the ships, pointing at them, as she counted, with her sword. She seemed a sort of fiend of destruction, and she called out to the birds, to encourage them to go. "Go!" said she, "without fear; you shall have abundance of prey. I am going too."

It is obvious that these dreams might as easily have been interpreted to portend death and destruction to their English foes as to the dreamers themselves. The soldiers were, however, inclined—in the state of mind which the season of the year, the threatening aspect of the skies, and the certain dangers of their distant expedition, produced—to apply the gloomy predictions which they imagined these dreams expressed, to themselves. Their chief, however, was of too desperate and determined a character to pay any regard to such influences. He set sail. His armament crossed the German Sea in safety, and joined Tostig on the coast of Scotland. The combined fleet moved slowly southward, along the shore, watching for an opportunity to land.

They reached, at length, the town of Scarborough, and landed to attack it. The inhabitants retired within the walls, shut the gates, and bid the invaders defiance. The town was situated under a hill, which rose in a steep acclivity upon one side. The story is, that the Norwegians went upon this hill, where they piled up an enormous heap of trunks and

The Norwegians at Scarborough.

branches of trees, with the interstices filled with stubble, dried bark, and roots, and other such combustibles, and then setting the whole mass on fire, they rolled it down into the town —a vast ball of fire, roaring and crackling more and more, by the fanning of its flames in the wind, as it bounded along. The intelligent reader will, of course, pause and hesitate, in considering how far to credit such a story. It is obviously impossible that any mere *pile*, however closely packed, could be made to roll. But it is, perhaps, not absolutely impossible that trunks of trees might be framed together, or fastened with wet thongs or iron chains, after being made in the form of a rude cylinder or ball, and filled with combustibles within, so as to retain its integrity in such a descent.

The account states that this strange method of bombardment was successful. The town was set on fire; the people surrendered. Tostig and the Norwegians plundered it, and then, embarking again in their ships, they continued their voyage.

The intelligence of this descent upon his northern coasts reached Harold in London toward the close of September, just as he was withdrawing his forces from the southern fron-

tier, as was related in the last chapter, under
the idea that the Norman invasion would probably be postponed until the spring; so that,
instead of sending his troops into their winter
quarters, he had to concentrate them again with
all dispatch, and march at the head of them to
the north, to avert this new and unexpected
danger.

While King Harold was thus advancing to
meet them, Tostig and his Norwegian allies entered the River Humber. Their object was to
reach the city of York, which had been Tostig's
former capital, and which was situated near
the River Ouse, a branch of the Humber. They
accordingly ascended the Humber to the mouth
of the Ouse, and thence up the latter river to a
suitable point of debarkation not far from York.
Here they landed and formed a great encampment. From this encampment they advanced
to the siege of the city. The inhabitants made
some resistance at first; but, finding that their
cause was hopeless, they offered to surrender,
and a treaty of surrender was finally concluded.
This negotiation was closed toward the evening
of the day, and Tostig and his confederate forces
were to be admitted on the morrow. They
therefore, feeling that their prize was secure,

withdrew to their encampment for the night,
and left the city to its repose.

It so happened that King Harold arrived that
very night, coming to the rescue of the city.
He expected to have found an army of besiegers
around the walls, but, instead of that, there was
nothing to intercept his progress up to the very
gates of the city. The inhabitants opened the
gates to receive him, and the whole detachment
which was marching under his command passed
in, while Tostig and his Norwegian allies were
sleeping quietly in their camp, wholly uncon-
scious of the great change which had thus taken
place in the situation of their affairs.

The next morning Tostig drew out a large
portion of the army, and formed them in array,
for the purpose of advancing to take possession
of the city. Although it was September, and
the weather had been cold and stormy, it happened that, on that morning, the sun came out
bright, and the air was calm, giving promise of
a warm day; and as the movement into the
city was to be a peaceful one—a procession, as
it were, and not a hostile march—the men were
ordered to leave their coats of mail and all their
heavy armor in camp, that they might march
the more unencumbered. While they were ad-

vancing in this unconcerned and almost defense-
less condition, they saw before them, on the
road leading to the city, a great cloud of dust
arising.   It was a strong body of King Harold's
troops coming out to attack them.   At first,
Tostig and the Norwegians were completely
lost and bewildered at the appearance of so unexpected a spectacle.   Very soon they could
see weapons glittering here and there, and banners flying.   A cry of " The enemy ! the enemy !" arose, and passed along their ranks, producing universal alarm.   Tostig and the Norwegian Harold halted their men, and marshaled
them hastily in battle array.   The English
Harold did the same, when he had drawn up
near to the front of the enemy ; both parties
then paused, and stood surveying one another.

Presently there was seen advancing from the
English side a squadron of twenty horsemen,
splendidly armed, and bearing a flag of truce.
They approached to within a short distance of
the Norwegian lines, when a herald, who was
among them, called out aloud for Tostig.   Tostig came forward in answer to the summons.
The herald then proclaimed to Tostig that his
brother did not wish to contend with him, but
desired, on the contrary, that they should live

A.D. 1066.] BATTLE OF HASTINGS.   223

Negotiations between Tostig and his brother.   The battle.

together in harmony. He offered him peace, therefore, if he would lay down his arms, and he promised to restore him his former possessions and honors.

Tostig seemed very much inclined to receive this proposition favorably. He paused and hesitated. At length he asked the messenger what terms King Harold would make with his friend and ally, the Norwegian Harold. "He shall have," replied the messenger, "seven feet of English ground for a grave. He shall have a little more than that, for he is taller than common men." "Then," replied Tostig, "tell my brother to prepare for battle. It shall never be said that I abandoned and betrayed my ally and friend."

The troop returned with Tostig's answer to Harold's lines, and the battle almost immediately began. Of course the most eager and inveterate hostility of the English army would be directed against the Norwegians and their king, whom they considered as foreign intruders, without any excuse or pretext for their aggression. It accordingly happened that, very soon after the commencement of the conflict, Harold the Norwegian fell, mortally wounded by an arrow in his throat. The English king then made new proposals to Tostig to cease the combat, and come to some terms of accommodation. But, in the mean time, Tostig had become himself incensed, and would listen to no overtures of peace. He continued the combat until he was himself killed. The remaining combatants in his army had now no longer any motive for resistance. Harold offered them a free passage to their ships, that they might return home in peace, if they would lay down their arms. They accepted the offer, retired on board their ships, and set sail. Harold then, having, in the mean time, heard of William's landing on the southern coast, set out on his return to the southward, to meet the more formidable enemy that menaced him there.

His army, though victorious, was weakened by the fatigues of the march, and by the losses suffered in the battle. Harold himself had been wounded, though not so severely as to prevent his continuing to exercise the command. He pressed on toward the south with great energy, sending messages on every side, into the surrounding country, on his line of march, calling upon the chieftains to arm themselves and their followers, and to come on with all possible dispatch, and join him. He hoped to advance so

rapidly to the southern coast as to surprise
William before he should have fully intrenched
himself in his camp, and without his being
aware of his enemy's approach. But William,
in order to guard effectually against surprise,
had sent out small reconnoitering parties of
horsemen on all the roads leading northward,
that they might bring him in intelligence of the
first approach of the enemy. Harold's advanced
guard met these parties, and saw them as they
drove rapidly back to the camp to give the
alarm. Thus the hope of surprising William
was disappointed. Harold found, too, by his
spies, as he drew near, to his utter dismay, that
William's forces were four times as numerous
as his own. It would, of course, be madness for
him to think of attacking an enemy in his in-
trenchments with such an inferior force. The
only alternative left him was either to retreat,
or else to take some strong position and fortify
himself there, in the hope of being able to resist
the invaders and arrest their advance, though
he was not strong enough to attack them.

Some of his counselors advised him not to
hazard a battle at all, but to fall back toward
London, carrying with him or destroying every
thing which could afford sustenance to Will-

28—15

226 WILLIAM THE CONQUEROR.

Advice of Harold's counselors.   He rejects it.

iam's army from the whole breadth of the land.
This would soon, they said, reduce William's
army to great distress for want of food, since it
would be impossible for him to transport supplies across the Channel for so vast a multitude.
Besides, they said, this plan would compel William, in the extremity to which be would be reduced, to make so many predatory excursions
among the more distant villages and towns, as
would exasperate the inhabitants, and induce
them to join Harold's army in great numbers to
repel the invasion.   Harold listened to these
counsels, but said, after consideration, that he
could never adopt such a plan.   He could not
be so derelict to his duty as to lay waste a country which he was under obligations to protect
and save, or compel his people to come to his
aid by exposing them, designedly, to the excesses and cruelties of so ferocious an enemy.

Harold determined, therefore, on giving William battle.   It was not necessary, however, for
him to attack the invader.   He perceived at
once that if he should take a strong position
and fortify himself in it, William must necessarily attack *him*, since a foreign army, just
landed in the country, could not long remain in-
active on the shore.   Harold accordingly chose

a position six or seven miles from William's camp, and fortified himself strongly there. Of course neither army was in sight of the other, or knew the numbers, disposition, or plans of the enemy. The country between them was, so far as the inhabitants were concerned, a scene of consternation and terror. No one knew at what point the two vast clouds of danger and destruction which were hovering near them would meet, or over what regions the terrible storm which was to burst forth when the hour of that meeting should come, would sweep in its destructive fury. The inhabitants, therefore, were every where flying in dismay, conveying away the aged and the helpless by any means which came most readily to hand; taking with them, too, such treasures as they could carry, and hiding, in rude and uncertain places of concealment, those which they were compelled to leave behind. The region, thus, which lay between the two encampments was rapidly becoming a solitude and a desolation, across which no communication was made, and no tidings passed to give the armies at the encampments intelligence of each other.

Harold had two brothers among the officers of his army, Gurth and Leofwin. Their con-

duct toward the king seems to have been of a
more fraternal character than that of Tostig,
who had acted the part of a rebel and an enemy.
Gurth and Leofwin, on the contrary, adhered
to his cause, and, as the hour of danger and the
great crisis which was to decide their fate drew
nigh, they kept close to his side, and evinced a
truly fraternal solicitude for his safety.　It was
they, specially, who had recommended to Harold to fall back on London, and not risk his life,
and the fate of his kingdom, on the uncertain
event of a battle.

As soon as Harold had completed his encampment, he expressed a desire to Gurth to ride
across the intermediate country and take a view
of William's lines.　Such an undertaking was
less dangerous then than it would be at the
present day; for now, such a reconnoitering
party would be discovered from the enemy's encampment, at a great distance, by means of
spy-glasses, and a twenty-four-pound shot or a
shell would be sent from a battery to blow the
party to pieces or drive them away.　The only
danger *then* was of being pursued by a detachment of horsemen from the camp, or surrounded
by an ambuscade.　To guard against these dangers, Harold and Gurth took the most powerful

and fleetest horses in the camp, and they called out a small but strong guard of well-selected men to escort them. Thus provided and attended, they rode over to the enemy's lines, and advanced so near that, from a small eminence to which they ascended, they could survey the whole scene of William's encampment: the palisades and embankments with which it was guarded, which extended for miles; the long lines of tents within; the vast multitude of soldiers; the knights and officers riding to and fro, glittering with steel; and the grand pavilion of the duke himself, with the consecrated banner of the cross floating above it. Harold was very much impressed with the grandeur of the spectacle.

After gazing on this scene for some time in silence, Harold said to Gurth that perhaps, after all, the policy of falling back would have been the wisest for them to adopt, rather than to risk a battle with so overwhelming a force as they saw before them. He did not know, he added, but that it would be best for them to change their plan, and adopt that policy now. Gurth said that it was too late. They had taken their stand, and now for them to break up their encampment and retire would be consid-

15

ered a retreat and not a maneuver, and it would discourage and dishearten the whole realm.

After surveying thus, as long as they desired to do so, the situation and extent of William's encampment, Harold's party returned to their own lines, still determined to make a stand there against the invaders, but feeling great doubt and despondency in respect to the result. Harold sent over, too, in the course of the day, some spies. The men whom he employed for this purpose were Normans by birth, and they could speak the French language. There were many Normans in England, who had come over in King Edward's time. These Norman spies could, of course, disguise themselves, and mingle, without attracting attention, among the thousands of workmen and camp followers that were going and coming continually around the grounds which William's army occupied. They did this so effectually, that they penetrated within the encampment without difficulty, examined every thing, and, in due time, returned to Harold with their report. They gave a formidable account of the numbers and condition of William's troops. There was a large corps of bowmen in the army, which had adopted a fashion of being shaven and shorn in

such a manner that the spies mistook them for
priests. They told Harold, accordingly, on their
return, that there were more *priests* in William's camp than there were soldiers in all his
army.

During this eventful day, William too sent
a body of horsemen across the country which
separated the two encampments, though his
emissaries were not spies, but embassadors,
with propositions for peace. William had no
wish to fight a battle, if what he considered as
rightfully his kingdom could be delivered to him
without it; and he determined to make one
final effort to obtain a peaceable surrender of
it, before coming to the dreadful resort of an
appeal to arms. He accordingly sent his embassy with *three* propositions to make to the
English king. The principal messenger in this
company was a monk, whose name was Maigrot.
He rode, with a proper escort and a flag of truce,
to Harold's lines. The propositions were these,
by accepting either of which the monk said
that Harold might avoid a battle. 1. That
Harold should surrender the kingdom to William, as he had solemnly sworn to do over the
sacred relics in Normandy. 2. That they should
both agree to refer the whole subject of contro-

versy between them to the pope, and abide by his decision. 3. That they should settle the dispute by single combat, the two claimants to the crown to fight a duel on the plain, in presence of their respective armies.

It is obvious that Harold could not accept either of these propositions. The first was to give up the whole point at issue. As for the second, the pope had already prejudged the case, and if it were to be referred to him, there could be no doubt that he would simply reaffirm his former decision. And in respect to single combat, the disadvantage on Harold's part would be as great in such a contest as it would be in the proposed arbitration. He was himself a man of comparatively slender form and of little bodily strength. William, on the other hand, was distinguished for his size, and for his extraordinary muscular energy. In a modern combat with fire-arms these personal advantages would be of no avail, but in those days, when the weapons were battle-axes, lances, and swords, they were almost decisive of the result. Harold therefore declined all William's propositions, and the monk returned.

William seems not to have been wholly discouraged by this failure of his first attempt at

negotiation, for he sent his embassage a second
time to make one more proposal.   It was, that
if Harold would consent to acknowledge William as King of England, William would assign
the whole territory to him and to his brother
Gurth, to hold *as provinces*, under William's
general sway.   Under this arrangement William would himself return to Normandy, making
the city of Rouen, which was his capital there,
the capital of the whole united realm.   To this
proposal Harold replied, that he could not, on
any terms, give up his rights as sovereign of England.   He therefore declined this proposal also.
He, however, now made a proposition in his
turn.   He was willing, he said, to compromise
the dispute, so far as it could be done by *the
payment of money*.   If William would abandon
his invasion and return to Normandy, giving
up his claims to the English crown, he would
pay him, he said, any sum of money that he
would name.

William could not accept this proposal.   He
was, as he believed, the true and rightful heir
to the throne of England, and there was a point
of honor involved, as well as a dictate of ambition to be obeyed, in insisting on the claim.
In the mean time, the day had passed, while

these fruitless negotiations had been pending. Night was coming on. William's officers and counselors began to be uneasy at the delay. They said that every hour new re-enforcements were coming into Harold's camp, while they themselves were gaining no advantage, and, consequently, the longer the battle was delayed, the less was the certainty of victory. So William promised them that he would attack King Harold in his camp the very next morning.

As the time for the great final struggle drew near, Harold's mind was oppressed more and more with a sense of anxiety and with foreboding fears. His brothers, too, were ill at ease. Their solicitude was increased by the recollection of Harold's oath, and of the awful sanctions with which they feared the sacred relics might have invested it. They were not sure that their brother's excuse for setting it aside would save him from the guilt and curse of perjury in the sight of Heaven. So they proposed, on the eve of the battle, that Harold himself should retire, and leave them to conduct the defense. "We can not deny," they said, "that you did take the oath ; and, notwithstanding the circumstances which seem to absolve you from the obligation, it is best to avoid, if possible, the

A.D. 1066.] BATTLE OF HASTINGS.   235

Night before the battle.   Scenes in Harold's camp.

open violation of it. It will be better, on the whole, for you to leave the army and go to London. You can aid very effectually in the defense of the kingdom by raising re-enforcements there. We will stay and encounter the actual battle. Heaven can not be displeased with us for so doing, for we shall be only discharging the duty incumbent on all, of defending their native land from foreign invasion."

Harold would not consent to adopt this plan. He could not retire himself, he said, at the hour of approaching danger, and leave his brothers and his friends exposed, when it was *his* crown for which they were contending.

Such were the circumstances of the two armies on the evening before the battle; and, of course, in such a state of things, the tendency of the minds of men would be, in Harold's camp, to gloom and despondency, and in William's, to confidence and exultation. Harold undertook, as men in his circumstances often do, to lighten the load which weighed upon his own heart and oppressed the spirits of his men, by feasting and wine. He ordered a plentiful supper to be served, and supplied his soldiers with abundance of drink; and it is said that his whole camp exhibited, during the whole night, one wide-spread scene of carousing and revelry, the troops being gathered every where in groups around their camp fires, some half stupefied, others quarreling, and others still singing national songs, and dancing with wild excitement, according to the various effects produced upon different constitutions by the intoxicating influence of beer and wine.

In William's camp there were witnessed very different scenes. There were a great many monks and ecclesiastics in the train of his army, and, on the night before the battle, they spent the time in saying masses, reading litanies and prayers, chanting anthems, and in other similar acts of worship, assisted by the soldiers, who gathered, in great congregations, for this wild worship, in the open spaces among the tents and around the camp fires. At length they all retired to rest, feeling an additional sense of safety in respect to the work of the morrow by having, as they supposed, entitled themselves, by their piety, to the protection of Heaven.

In the morning, too, in William's camp, the first thing done was to convene the army for a grand celebration of mass. It is a curious illustration of the mingling of the religious, or, perhaps, we ought rather to say, the superstitious

sentiment of the times, with the spirit of war,
that the bishop who officiated in this solemn
service of the mass wore a coat of mail under
his pontifical attire, and an attendant stood by
his side, while he was offering his prayers, with
a steel-pointed spear in his hand, ready for the
martial prelate to assume as soon as the service
should be ended. Accordingly, when the religious duty was performed, the bishop threw
off his surplice, took his spear, and mounting
his white charger, which was also all saddled
and bridled beside him, he headed a brigade of
horse, and rode on to the assault of the enemy.

William himself mounted a very magnificent
war-horse from Spain, a present which he had
formerly received from one of his wealthy barons.
The name of the horse was Bayard. From
William's neck were suspended some of the
most sacred of the relics over which Harold had
taken his false oath. He imagined that there
would be some sort of charm in them, to protect his life, and to make the judgment of
Heaven more sure against the perjurer. The
standard which the pope had blessed was borne
by his side by a young standard bearer, who
was very proud of the honor. An older soldier,
however, on whom the care of this standard

officially devolved, had asked to be excused
from carrying it. He wished, he said, to do
his work that day with the *sword*. While making these preliminary arrangements for going
into battle, William, with the party around him,
stood upon a gentle eminence in the middle of
the camp, and in sight of the whole army.
Every one was struck with admiration at the
splendid figure which their commander made—
his large and well-formed limbs covered with
steel, and his horse, whose form was as noble
as that of his master, prancing restlessly, as if
impatient for the battle to begin.

When all were ready, the Norman army advanced gayly and joyously to attack the English lines; but the gayety and joyousness of
the scene soon disappeared, as corps after corps
got fairly engaged in the awful work of the day.
For ten long hours there reigned over the whole
field one wide-spread scene o havoc and death—
every soul among all those countless thousands
delivered up to the supreme dominion of the most
dreadful passions, excited to a perfect phrensy of hatred, rage, and revenge, and all either
mercilessly killing others, or dying themselves
in agony and despair. When night came, the
Normans were every where victorious. They

were in full possession of the field, and they rode triumphantly to and fro through Harold's camp, leaping their horses over the bodies of the dead and dying which covered the ground. Those of King Harold's followers that had escaped the slaughter of the day fled in hopeless confusion toward the north, where the flying masses strewed the roads for miles with the bodies of men who sank down on the way, spent with wounds or exhausted by fatigue.

In the morning, William marshaled his men on the field, and called over the names of the officers and men, as they had been registered in Normandy, for the purpose of ascertaining who were killed. While this melancholy ceremony was going on, two monks came in, sent from the remains of the English army, and saying that King Harold was missing, and that it was rumored that he had been slain. If so, his body must be lying somewhere, they said, upon the field, and they wished for permission to make search for it. The permission was granted. With the aid of some soldiers they began to explore the ground, turning over and examining every lifeless form which, by the dress or the armor, might seem to be possibly the king's. Their search was for a long time vain; the

240 WILLIAM THE CONQUEROR.

Final subjugation of the island.   William crowned at Westminster.

ghastly faces of the dead were so mutilated and changed that nobody could be identified. At length, however, a woman who had been in Harold's family, and knew his person more intimately than they, found and recognized the body, and the monks and the soldiers carried it away.

The battle of Hastings sealed and settled the controversy in respect to the English crown. It is true that the adherents of Harold, and also those of Edgar Atheling, made afterward various efforts to rally their forces and recover the kingdom, but in vain. William advanced to London, fortified himself there, and made excursions from that city as a centre until he reduced the island to his sway. He was crowned at length, at Westminster Abbey, with great pomp and parade. He sent for Matilda to come and join him, and instated her in his palace as Queen of England. He confiscated the property of all the English nobles who had fought against him, and divided it among the Norman chieftains who had aided him in the invasion. He made various excursions to and from Normandy himself, being received every where throughout his dominions, on both sides the

Channel, with the most distinguished honors. In a word, he became, in the course of a few years after he landed, one of the greatest and most powerful potentates on the globe. How far all his riches and grandeur were from making him happy, will appear in the following chapter.

• 28—16

CHAPTER XI.

PRINCE ROBERT'S REBELLION.

AMBITIOUS men, who devote their time and attention, through all the early years of life, to their personal and political aggrandizement, have little time to appropriate to the government and education of their children, and their later years are often embittered by the dissipation and vice, or by the unreasonable exactions of their sons.   At least it was so in William's case.   By the time that his public enemies were subdued, and he found himself undisputed master both of his kingdom and his duchy, his peace and happiness were destroyed, and the tranquillity of his whole realm was disturbed by a terrible family quarrel.

The name of his oldest son was Robert.   He was fourteen years old when his father set off on his invasion of England.   At that time he was a sort of spoiled child, having been his mother's favorite, and, as such, always greatly indulged by her.   When William went away, it will be recollected that he appointed Matilda regent, to govern Normandy during his absence. This boy was also named in the regency, so that he was nominally associated with his mother, and he considered himself, doubtless, as the more important personage of the two. In a word, while William was engaged in England, prosecuting his conquests there, Robert was growing up in Normandy a vain, self-conceited, and ungovernable young man.

His father, in going back and forth between England and Normandy, often came into conflict with his son, as usual in such cases. In these contests Matilda took sides with the son. William's second son, whose name was William Rufus, was jealous of his older brother, and was often provoked by the overbearing and imperious spirit which Robert displayed. William Rufus thus naturally adhered to the father's part in the family feud. William Rufus was as rough and turbulent in spirit as Robert, but he had not been so indulged. He possessed, therefore, more self-control; he knew very well how to suppress his propensities, and conceal the unfavorable aspects of his character when in the presence of his father.

There was a third brother, named Henry. He was of a more quiet and inoffensive charac-

244 WILLIAM THE CONQUEROR.

William's son Henry.   Robert nicknamed Short Boots.

ter, and avoided taking an active part in the
quarrel, except so far as William Rufus led
him on. He was William Rufus's friend and
companion, and, as such, Robert considered him
as his enemy. All, in fact, except Matilda,
were against Robert, who looked down, in a
haughty and domineering manner—as the oldest son and heir is very apt to do in rich and
powerful families—upon the comparative insignificance of his younger brethren. The king,
instead of restraining this imperious spirit in
his son, as he might, perhaps, have done by a
considerate and kind, and, at the same time,
decisive exercise of authority, teased and tor-
mented him by sarcasms and petty vexations.
Among other instances of this, he gave him the
nickname of *Short Boots*, because he was of inferior stature. As Robert was, however, at this
time of full age, he was stung to the quick at
having such a stigma attached to him by his
father, and his bosom burned with secret sentiments of resentment and revenge.

He had, besides, other causes of complaint
against his father, more serious still. When he
was a very young child, his father, according to
the custom of the times, had espoused him to
the daughter and heiress of a neighboring earl,

a child like himself. Her name was Margaret.
The earldom which this little Margaret was to
inherit was Maine. It was on the frontiers of
Normandy, and it was a rich and valuable possession. It was a part of the stipulation of the
marriage contract that the young bride's domain was to be delivered to the father of the
bridegroom, to be held by him until the bridegroom should become of age, and the marriage
should be fully consummated. In fact, the getting possession of this rich inheritance, with a
prospect of holding it so many years, was very
probably the principal end which William had
in view in contracting for a matrimonial union
so very premature.

If this was, in reality, William's plan, it resulted, in the end, even more favorably than he
had anticipated; for the little heiress died a
short time after her inheritance was put into
the possession of her father-in-law. There was
nobody to demand a restoration of it, and so
William continued to hold it until his son, the
bridegroom, became of age. Robert then demanded it, contending that it was justly his.
William refused to surrender it. He maintained that what had passed between his son in his
infancy, and the little Margaret, was not a mar-

16

riage, but only a betrothment—a contract for a future marriage, which was to take place when the parties were of age—that, since Margaret's death prevented the consummation of the union, Robert was never her husband, and could not, consequently, acquire the rights of a husband. The lands, therefore, ought manifestly, he said, to remain in the hands of her guardian, and whatever rights any other persons might have, claiming to succeed Margaret as her natural heirs, it was plain that his son could have no title whatever.

However satisfactory this reasoning might be to the mind of William, Robert was only exasperated by it. He looked upon the case as one of extreme injustice and oppression on the part of his father, who, not content, he said, with his own enormous possessions, must add to them by robbing his own son. In this opinion Robert's mother, Matilda, agreed with him. As for William Rufus and Henry, they paid little attention to the argument, but were pleased with the result of it, and highly enjoyed their brother's vexation and chagrin in not being able to get possession of his earldom.

There was another very serious subject of dispute between Robert and his father. It has

already been stated, that when the duke set
out on his expedition for the invasion of England, he left Matilda and Robert together in
charge of the duchy. At the commencement
of the period of his absence Robert was very
young, and the actual power rested mainly in
his mother's hands. As he grew older, however, he began to exercise an increasing influence and control. In fact, as he was himself
ambitious and aspiring, and his mother indul-
gent, the power passed very rapidly into his
hands. It was eight years from the time that
William left Normandy before his power was
so far settled and established in England that
he could again take the affairs of his original
realm into his hands. He had left Robert, at
that time, a mere boy of fourteen, who, though
rude and turbulent in character, was still politically powerless. He found him, on his return,
a man of twenty-two, ruder and more turbulent
than before, and in the full possession of political power. This power, too, he found him
very unwilling to surrender.

In fact, when William came to receive back
the province of Normandy again, Robert almost
refused to surrender it. He said that his father
had always promised him the duchy of Nor-

mandy as his domain so soon as he should become of age, and he claimed now the fulfillment of this promise. Besides, he said that, now that his father was King of England, his former realm was of no consequence to him. It did not add sensibly to his influence or his power, and he might, therefore, without suffering any sensible loss himself, grant it to his son. William, on his part, did not acknowledge the force of either of these arguments. He would not admit that he had ever promised Normandy to his son; and as to voluntarily relinquishing any part of his possessions, he had no faith in the policy of a man's giving up his power or his property to his children until they were justly entitled to inherit it by his death; at any rate, he should not do it. He had no idea, as he expressed it, "of putting off his clothes before he was going to bed."

The irritation and ill-will which these dissensions produced grew deeper and more inveterate every day, though the disagreement had been thus far a private and domestic dispute, confined, in its influence, to the king's immediate household. An occasion, however, now occurred, on which the private family feud broke out into an open public quarrel. The circumstances were these:

King William had a castle in Normandy, at a place called L'Aigle. He was spending some time there, in the year 1076, with his court and family. One day William Rufus and Henry were in one of the upper apartments of the castle, playing with dice, and amusing themselves, in company with other young men of the court, in various ways. There was a window in the apartment leading out upon a balcony, from which one might look down upon the court-yard of the castle below. Robert was in this court-yard with some of *his* companions, walking there in an irritated state of mind, which had been produced by some previous disputes with his brothers. William Rufus looked down from the balcony and saw him, and by way, perhaps, of quenching his anger, poured some water down upon him. The deed changed the suppressed and silent irritation in Robert's heart to a perfect phrensy of rage and revenge. He drew his sword and sprang to the stair-case. He uttered loud and terrible imprecations as he went, declaring that he would kill the author of such an insult, even if he *was* his brother. The court-yard was, of course, immediately filled with shouts and exclamations of alarm, and every body pressed forward toward the room from which the water had been thrown, some to witness, and some to prevent the affray.

The king himself, who happened to be in that part of the castle at the time, was one of the number. He reached the apartment just in time to interpose between his sons, and prevent the commission of the awful crime of fratricide. As it was, he found it extremely difficult to part the ferocious combatants. It required all his paternal authority, and not a little actual force, to arrest the affray. He succeeded, however, at length, with the help of the by-standers, in parting his sons, and Robert, out of breath, and pale with impotent rage, was led away.

Robert considered his father as taking sides against him in this quarrel, and he declared that he could not, and would not, endure such treatment any longer. He found some sympathy in the conversation of his mother, to whom he went immediately with bitter complainings. She tried to soothe and quiet his wounded spirit, but he would not be pacified. He spent the afternoon and evening in organizing a party of wild and desperate young men from among the nobles of the court, with a view of raising a rebellion against his father, and get-

ting possession of Normandy by force. They
kept their designs profoundly secret, but prepared
to leave L'Aigle that night, to go and seize
Rouen, the capital, which they hoped to surprise into a surrender. Accordingly, in the
middle of the night, the desperate troop mounted their horses and rode away. In the morning
the king found that they were gone, and he
sent an armed force after them. Their plan of
surprising Rouen failed. The king's detachment overtook them, and, after a sharp contest,
succeeded in capturing a few of the rebels,
though Robert himself, accompanied by some
of the more desperate of his followers, escaped
over the frontier into a neighboring province,
where he sought refuge in the castle of one of
his father's enemies.

This result, as might have been expected,
filled the mind of Matilda with anxiety and
distress. A civil war between her husband and
her son was now inevitable; and while every
consideration of prudence and of duty required
her to espouse the father's cause, her maternal
love, a principle stronger far, in most cases,
than prudence and duty combined, drew her
irresistibly toward her son. Robert collected
around him all the discontented and desperate

spirits of the realm, and for a long time continued to make his father infinite trouble.
Matilda, while she forbore to advocate his cause
openly in the presence of the king, kept up a
secret communication with him. She sent him
information and advice from time to time, and
sometimes supplies, and was thus, technically,
guilty of a great crime—the crime of maintaining a treasonable correspondence with a rebel.
In a moral point of view, however, her conduct
may have been entirely right; at any rate, its
influence was very salutary, for she did all in
her power to restrain both the father and the
son; and by the influence which she thus exerted, she doubtless mitigated very much the
fierceness of the struggle.

Of course, the advantage, in such a civil war
as this, would be wholly on the side of the
sovereign. William had all the power and resources of the kingdom in his own hands—the
army, the towns, the castles, the treasures.
Robert had a troop of wild, desperate, and unmanageable outlaws, without authority, without money, without a sense of justice on their
side. He gradually became satisfied that the
contest was vain. In proportion as the activity
of the hostilities diminished, Matilda became

more and more open in her efforts to restrain it,
and to allay the animosity on either side. She
succeeded, finally, in inducing Robert to lay
down his arms, and then brought about an interview between the parties, in hopes of a peaceful settlement of the quarrel.

It appeared very soon, however, at this interview, that there was no hope of any thing
like a real and cordial reconciliation. Though
both the father and son had become weary of
the unnatural war which they had waged
against each other, yet the ambitious and selfish desires on both sides, in which the contest
had originated, remained unchanged. Robert
began the conference by imperiously demanding
of his father the fulfillment of his promise to
give him the government of Normandy. His
father replied by reproaching him with his unnatural and wicked rebellion, and warned him
of the danger he incurred, in imitating the example of Absalom, of sharing that wretched
rebel's fate. Robert rejoined that he did not
come to meet his father for the sake of hearing
a sermon preached. He had had enough of
sermons, he said, when he was a boy, studying
grammar. He wanted his father to do him
justice, not preach to him. The king said that

he should never divide his dominions, while he lived, with any one; and added, notwithstanding what Robert had contemptuously said about sermons, that the Scripture declared that a house divided against itself could not stand. He then proceeded to reproach and incriminate the prince in the severest manner for his disloyalty as a subject, and his undutifulness and ingratitnde as a son. It was intolerable, he said, that a son should become the rival and bitterest enemy of his father, when it was to him that he owed, not merely all that he enjoyed, but his very existence itself.

These reproaches were probably uttered in an imperious and angry manner, and with that spirit of denunciation which only irritates the accused and arouses his resentment, instead of awakening feelings of penitence and contrition. At any rate, the thought of his filial ingratitude, as his father presented it, produced no relenting in Robert's mind. He abruptly terminated the interview, and went out of his father's presence in a rage.

In spite of all his mother's exertions and entreaties, he resolved to leave the country once more. He said he would rather be an exile, and wander homeless in foreign lands, than to

remain in his father's court, and be treated in
so unjust and ignominious a manner, by one
who was bound by the strongest possible obligations to be his best and truest friend. Matilda could not induce him to change this de-
termination ; and, accordingly, taking with him
a few of the most desperate and dissolute of his
companions, he went northward, crossed the
frontier, and sought refuge in Flanders. Flanders, it will be recollected, was Matilda's native
land. Her brother was the Earl of Flanders at
this time. The earl received young Robert
very cordially, both for his sister's sake, and
also, probably, in some degree, as a means of
petty hostility against King William, his powerful neighbor, whose glory and good fortune
he envied.

Robert had not the means or the resources
necessary for renewing an open war with his
father, but his disposition to do this was as
strong as ever, and he began immediately to
open secret communications and correspondence
with all the nobles and barons in Normandy
whom he thought disposed to espouse his cause.
He succeeded in inducing them to make secret
contributions of funds to supply his pecuniary
wants, of course promising to repay them with

ample grants and rewards so soon as he should obtain his rights. He maintained similar communications, too, with Matilda, though she kept them very profoundly secret from her husband.

Robert had other friends besides those whom he found thus furtively in Normandy. The King of France himself was much pleased at the breaking out of this terrible feud in the family of his neighbor, who, from being his dependent and vassal, had become, by his conquest of England, his great competitor and rival in the estimation of mankind. Philip was disposed to rejoice at any occurrences which tended to tarnish William's glory, or which threatened a division and diminution of his power. He directed his agents, therefore, both in Normandy and in Flanders, to encourage and promote the dissension by every means in their power. He took great care not to commit himself by any open and positive promises of aid, and yet still he contrived, by a thousand indirect means, to encourage Robert to expect it. Thus the mischief was widened and extended, while yet nothing effectual was done toward organizing an insurrection. In fact, Robert had neither the means nor the mental capacity necessary for maturing and carrying into effect any

actual plan of rebellion. In the mean time,
months passed away, and as nothing effectual
was done, Robert's adherents in Normandy became gradually discouraged. They ceased their
contributions, and gradually forgot their absent
and incompetent leader. Robert spent his time
in dissipation and vice, squandering in feasts
and in the company of abandoned men and
women the means which his followers sent him
to enable him to prepare for the war; and when,
at last, these supplies failed him, he would have
been reduced gradually to great distress and
destitution, were it not that one faithful and
devoted friend still adhered to him. That friend
was his mother.

Matilda knew very well that whatever she
did for her absent son must be done in the most
clandestine manner, and this required much
stratagem and contrivance on her part. She
was aided, however, in her efforts at concealment by her husband's absence. He was now
for a time in England, having been called there
by some pressing demands of public duty. He
left a great minister of state in charge of Nor,
mandy, whose vigilance Matilda thought it
would be comparatively easy to elude. She
sent to Robert, in Flanders, first her own pri-

28—17

vate funds.   Then she employed for this purpose a portion of such public funds as came
into her hands.   The more she sent, however,
the more frequent and imperious were Robert's
demands for fresh supplies.   The resources of a
mother, whether great or small, are always soon
exhausted by the insatiable requirements of a
dissolute and profligate son.   When Matilda's
money was gone, she sold her jewels, then her
more expensive clothes, and, finally, such objects of value, belonging to herself or to her
husband, as could be most easily and privately
disposed of.   The minister, who was very faithful and watchful in the discharge of his duties,
observed indications that something mysterious
was going on.   His suspicions were aroused.
He watched Matilda's movements, and soon discovered the truth.   He sent information to
William.   William could not believe it possible that his minister's surmises could be true;
for William was simply a statesman and a soldier, and had very inadequate ideas of the ab-
sorbing and uncontrollable power which is exercised by the principle of maternal love.

He, however, determined immediately to take
most efficient measures to ascertain the truth.
He returned to Normandy, and there he suc-

ceeded in intercepting one of Matilda's messengers on his way to Flanders, with communications and money for Robert. The name of this
messenger was Sampson. William seized the
money and the letters, and sent the messenger
to one of his castles, to be shut up in a dun-
geon. Then, with the proofs of guilt which he
had thus obtained, he went, full of astonishment and anger, to find Matilda, and to up-
braid her, as he thought she deserved, for her
base and ungrateful betrayal of her husband.

The reproaches which he addressed to her
were bitter and stern, though they seem to have
been spoken in a tone of sorrow rather than of
anger. "I am sure," he said, "I have ever
been to you a faithful and devoted husband. I
do not know what more you could have desired
than I have done. I have loved you with a sincere and true affection. I have honored you.
I have placed you in the highest positions, in-
trusting you repeatedly with large shares of my
own sovereign power. I have confided in you
—committing my most essential and vital interests to your charge. And now this is the
return. You employ the very position, and
power, and means which your confiding husband has put into your hands, to betray him in

the most cruel way, and to aid and encourage his worst and most dangerous enemy."

To these reproaches Matilda attempted no reply, except to plead the irresistible impetuosity and strength of her maternal love. "I could not bear," she said, "to leave Robert in distress and suffering while I had any possible means of relieving him. He is my child. I think of him all the time. I love him more than my life. I solemnly declare to you, that if he were now dead, and I could restore him to life by dying for him, I would most gladly do it. How, then, do you suppose that I could possibly live here in abundance and luxury, while he was wandering homeless, in destitution and want, and not try to relieve him? Whether it is right or wrong for me to feel so, I do not know; but this I know, I *must* feel so: I can not help it. He is our first-born son; I can not abandon him."

William went away from the presence of Matilda full of resentment and anger. Of course he could do nothing in respect to her but reproach her, but he determined that the unlucky Sampson should suffer severely for the crime. He sent orders to the castle where he lay immured, requiring that his eyes should be

put out.   Matilda, however, discovered the danger which threatened her messenger in time to
send him warning.   He contrived to make his
escape, and fled to a certain monastery which
was under Matilda's special patronage and
charge.   A monastery was, in those days, a
sanctuary into which the arm even of the most
despotic authority scarcely dared to intrude in
pursuit of its victim.   To make the safety
doubly sure, the abbot proposed that the trem-
bling fugitive should join their order and become a monk.   Sampson was willing to do any
thing to save his life.   The operation of putting
out the eyes was very generally fatal, so that
he considered his life at stake.   He was, accordingly, shaven and shorn, and clothed in the
monastic garb.   He assumed the vows of the
órder, and entered, with his brother monks,
upon the course of fastings, penances, and prayers which pertained to his new vocation; and
William left him to pursue it in peace.

Things went on worse instead of better after
this discovery of the mother's participation in
the councils of the son.   Either through the aid
which his mother had rendered, or by other
means, there seemed to be a strong party in
and out of Normandy who were inclined to es-

17

pouse Robert's cause. His friends, at length, raised a very considerable army, and putting him at the head of it, they advanced to attack Rouen. The king, greatly alarmed at this danger, collected all the forces that he could command, and went to meet his rebel son. William Rufus accompanied his father, intending to fight by his side; while Matilda, in an agony of terror and distress, remained, half distracted, within her castle walls—as a wife and mother might be expected to be, on the approach of a murderous conflict between her husband and her son. The thought that one of them might, perhaps, be actually killed by the other, filled her with dismay.

And, in fact, this dreadful result came very near being realized. Robert, in the castle at L'Aigle, had barely been prevented from destroying his brother, and now, on the plain of Archembraye, where this battle was fought, his father *fell*, and was very near being killed, by his hand. In the midst of the fight, while the horsemen were impetuously charging each other in various parts of the field, all so disguised by their armor that no one could know the individual with whom he was contending, Robert encountered a large and powerful knight, and

drove his lance through his armor into his arm.
Through the shock of the encounter and the
faintness produced by the agony of the wound,
the horseman fell to the ground, and Robert
perceived, by the voice with which his fallen
enemy cried out in his pain and terror, that it
was his father that he had thus pierced with
his steel. At the same moment, the wounded
father, in looking at his victorious antagonist,
recognized his son. He cursed his unnatural
enemy with a bitter and terrible malediction.
Robert was shocked and terrified at what he
had done. He leaped from his horse, knelt
down by the side of his father, and called for
aid. The king, distracted by the anguish of
his wound, and by the burning indignation and
resentment which raged in his bosom against
the unnatural hostility which inflicted it, turned
away from his son, and refused to receive any
succor from him.

Besides the misfortune of being unhorsed
and wounded, the battle itself went that day
against the king. Robert's army remained
masters of the field. William Rufus was
wounded too, as well as his father. Matilda
was overwhelmed with distress and mental anguish at the result. She could not endure the

idea of allowing so unnatural and dreadful a struggle to go on. She begged her husband, with the most earnest importunities and with many tears, to find some way of accommodating the dispute. Her nights were sleepless, her days were spent in weeping, and her health and strength were soon found to be wasting very rapidly away. She was emaciated, wan, and pale, and it was plain that such distress, if long continued, would soon bring her to the grave.

Matilda's intercessions at length prevailed. The king sent for his son, and, after various negotiations, some sort of compromise was effected. The armies were disbanded, peace was restored, and Robert and his father once more seemed to be friends. Soon after this, William, having a campaign to make in the north of England, took Robert with him as one of the generals in his army.

CHAPTER XII.

THE CONCLUSION.

FROM the time of the battle of Hastings, which took place in 1066, to that of William's death, which occurred in 1087, there intervened a period of about twenty years, during which the great monarch reigned over his extended dominions with a very despotic sway, though not without a large share of the usual dangers, difficulties, and struggles attending such a rule. He brought over immense numbers of Normans from Normandy into England, and placed all the military and civil power of the empire in their hands; and he relied almost entirely upon the superiority of his physical force for keeping the country in subjugation to his sway. It is true, he maintained that he was the rightful heir to the English crown, and that, consequently, the tenure by which he held it was the right of inheritance, and not the right of conquest; and he professed to believe that the people of England generally admitted his claim. This was, in fact, to a considerable ex-

tent, true. At least there was probably a large
part of the population who believed William's
right to the crown superior to that of Harold,
whom he had deposed. Still, as William was
by birth, and education, and language a foreigner, and as all the friends and followers who attended him, and, in fact, almost the whole of
the army, on which he mainly relied for the
preservation of his power, were foreigners too
—wearing a strange dress, and speaking in an
unknown tongue—the great mass of the English people could not but feel that they were
under a species of foreign subjugation. Quarrels were therefore continually breaking out between them and their Norman masters, resulting in fierce and bloody struggles, on their part,
to get free. These rebellions were always effectually put down; but when quelled in one
quarter they soon broke out in another, and
they kept William and his forces almost always
employed.

But William was not a mere warrior. He
was well aware that the permanence and sta-
bility of his own and his successor's sway in
England would depend finally upon the kind
of basis on which the civil institutions of the
country should rest, and on the proper consolida-

tion and adjustment of the administrative and judicial functions of the realm. In the intervals of his campaigns, therefore, William devoted a great deal of time and attention to this subject, and he evinced a most profound and statesmanlike wisdom and sagacity in his manner of treating it.

He had, in fact, a Herculean task to perform —a double task—viz., to amalgamate two *nations*, and also to fuse and merge two *languages* into one. He was absolutely compelled, by the circumstances under which he was placed, to grapple with both these vast undertakings. If, at the time when, in his park at Rouen, he first heard of Harold's accession, he had supposed that there was a party in England in his favor strong enough to allow of his proceeding there alone, or with a small Norman attendance, so that he might rely mainly on the English themselves for his accession to the throne, the formidable difficulties which, as it was, he had subsequently to encounter, would all have been saved. But there was no such party—at least there was no evidence that there was one of sufficient strength to justify him in trusting himself to it. It seemed to him, then, that if he undertook to gain posses-

sion of the English throne at all, he must rely
entirely on the force which he could take with
him from Normandy. To make this reliance
effectual, the force so taken must be an overwhelming one. Then, if Normans in great
numbers were to go to England for the purpose
of putting him upon the English throne, they
must be rewarded, and so vast a number of
candidates for the prizes of honor and wealth
could be satisfied only in England, and by con-
fiscations there. His possessions in Normandy
would obviously be insufficient for such a purpose. It was evident, moreover, that if a large
number of Norman adventurers were placed in
stations of trust and honor, and charged with
civil offices and administrative functions all
over England, they would form a sort of class
by themselves, and would be looked upon with
jealousy and envy by the original inhabitants,
and that there was no hope of maintaining
them safely in their position except by making
the class as numerous and as strong as possible.
In a word, William saw very clearly that, while
it would have been very well, if it had been
possible, for him to have brought *no* Normans
to England, it was clearly best, since so many
must go, to contrive every means to swell and

The British realm Normanized.   O yes! O yes! O yes!

increase the number. It was one of those cases where, being obliged to go far, it is best to go farther; and William resolved on thoroughly *Normanizing*, so to speak, the whole British realm. This enormous undertaking he accomplished fully and permanently; and the institutions of England, the lines of family descent, the routine of judicial and administrative business, and the very language of the realm, retain the Norman characteristics which he ingrafted into them to the present day.

It gives us a feeling akin to that of sublimity to find, even in our own land, and in the most remote situations of it, the lingering relics of the revolutions and deeds of these early ages, still remaining, like a faint ripple rolling gently upon a beach in a deep and secluded bay, which was set in motion, perhaps, at first, as one of the mountainous surges of a wintery storm in the most distant seas. For example, if we enter the most humble court in any remote and newly-settled country in the American forests, a plain and rustic-looking man will call the equally rustic-looking assembly to order by rapping his baton, the only symbol of his office, on the floor, and calling out, in words mystic and meaningless to him, "O yes! O yes! O

yes!"*   He little thinks that he is obeying a
behest of William the Conqueror, issued eight
hundred years ago, ordaining that his native
tongue should be employed in the courts of England.   The irresistible progress of improve-
ment and reform have gradually displaced the
intruding language again—except so far as it
has become merged and incorporated with the
common language of the country—from all the
ordinary forms of legal proceedings.   It lingers
still, however, as it were, on the threshold, in
this call to order; and as it is harmless there,
the spirit of conservatism will, perhaps, preserve
for it this last place of refuge for a thousand
years to come, and "*O yes*" will be the phrase
for ordaining silence by many generations of
officers, who will, perhaps, never have heard of
the authority whose orders they unwittingly
obey.

The work of incorporating the Norman and
English families with one another, and fusing
the two languages into one, required about a
century for its full accomplishment; and when
at last it was accomplished, the people of England were somewhat puzzled to know whether

* Oyez! Oyez! Oyez! Norman French for Hearken!
hearken! hearken!

they ought to feel proud of William's exploits in the conquest of England, or humiliated by them. So far as they were themselves descended from the Normans, the conquest was one of the glorious deeds of their ancestors. So far as they were of English parentage, it would seem to be incumbent on them to mourn over their fathers' defeat. It is obvious that from such a species of perplexity as this there was no escape, and it has accordingly continued to embarrass the successive generations of Englishmen down to the present day. The Norman Conquest occupies, therefore, a very uncertain and equivocal position in English history, the various modern writers who look back to it now being hardly able to determine whether they are to regard it as a mortifying subjugation which their ancestors suffered, or a glorious victory which they gained.

One of the great measures of William's reign, and one, in fact, for which it has been particularly famous in modern times, was a grand census or registration of the kingdom, which the Conqueror ordered with a view of having on record a perfect enumeration and description of all the real and personal property in the kingdom. This grand national survey was made in

1078. The result was recorded in two volumes of different sizes, which were called the Great and the Little Domesday Book. These books are still preserved, and are to this day of the very highest authority in respect to all questions touching ancient rights of property. One is a folio, and the other a quarto volume. The records are written on vellum, in a close, abridged, and, to ordinary readers, a perfectly unintelligible character. The language is Latin; but a modern Latin scholar, without any means other than an inspection of the work, would be utterly unable to decipher it. In fact, though the character is highly wrought, and in some respects elegant, the whole style and arrangement of the work is pretty nearly on a par, in respect to scientific skill, with Queen Emma's designs upon the Bayeux tapestry. About half a century ago, copies of these works were printed, by means of type made to represent the original character. But these printed editions were found unintelligible and useless until copious indexes were prepared, and published to accompany them, at great expense of time and labor.

Some little idea of the character and style of this celebrated record may be obtained from the following specimen, which is as faithful an imitation of the original as any ordinary typography will allow:

In Brixistan Hund'.

Rex ten Bermundesye. heraldᵒ tenuit. Tc se def'd p. xiii. hid. mᵒ p. xii. hid. Tra. e. viii. car. In dnio. e una car. 7 xxv. villi 7 xxxiii. bord cu. un. car.

Ibi nova 7 pulchra eccla. 7 xx. ac pᵃ ti. Silba! v. porc de pasnag:

The passage, deciphered and expressed in full, stands thus — the letters omitted in the original, above, being supplied in italics:

IN BRIXISTAN HUNDredo.

Rex ten*et* BERMUNDESYE. Herald*us* com*es* tenuit. T*unc* se def*end*eba*t pro* xiii. hid*is*, mod*o pro* xii. hid*is*. Terra es*t* viii. carr*uc*a*tarum*. In d*o*minio e*st* una carr*uc*ata et xxv. vill*ani* et xxxiii. bord*arii* cum una carr*uc*ata. Ibi nova et pulchra eccl*esia*, et xx. ac*ræ* prati. Silva v. porc*is* de pasnag*io*.

The English translation is as follows:

In Brixistan Hundred.

The king holds BERMUNDESYE. Earl HERALD held it [before]. At that time it was rated at thirteen hides; now, at twelve. The arable land is eight carrucates [*or* plow-lands]. There is one carrucate in demesne, and twenty-five villans, and thirty-three bordars, with one carrucate. There is a new and handsome church, with twenty acres of meadow, and woodland for five hogs in pasnage [pasturage] time.

But we must pass on to the conclusion of the story. About the year 1082, Queen Matilda's

health began seriously to decline. She was
harassed by a great many anxieties and cares
connected with the affairs of state which devolved upon her, and arising from the situation
of her family : these anxieties produced great
dejection of spirits, and aggravated, if they did
not wholly cause, her bodily disease. She was at
this time in Normandy. One great source of
her mental suffering was her anxiety in respect
to one of her daughters, who, as well as herself, was declining in health. Forgetting her
own danger in her earnest desires for the welfare of her child, she made a sort of pilgrimage
to a monastery which contained the shrine of
a certain saint, who, as she imagined, had power to save her daughter. She laid a rich present on the shrine ; she offered before it most
earnest prayers, imploring, with tears of bitter
grief, the intercession of the saint, and mani-
festing every outward symbol of humility and
faith. She took her place in the religious services of the monastery, and conformed to its
usages, as if she had been in the humblest private station. But all was in vain. The health
of her beloved daughter continued to fail, until
at length she died ; and Matilda, growing herself more feeble, and almost broken hearted

through grief, shut herself up in the palace at Caen.

It was in the same palace which William had built, within his monastery, many long years before, at the time of their marriage. Matilda looked back to that period, and to the buoyant hopes and bright anticipations of power, glory, and happiness which then filled her heart, with sadness and sorrow. The power and the glory had been attained, and in a measure tenfold greater than she had imagined, but the happiness had never come. Ambition had been contending unceasingly for twenty years, among all the branches of her family, against domestic peace and love. She possessed, herself, an aspiring mind, but the principles of maternal and conjugal love were stronger in her heart than those of ambition; and yet she was compelled to see ambition bearing down and destroying love in all its forms every where around her. Her last days were embittered by the breaking out of new contests between her husband and her son.

Matilda sought for peace and comfort in multiplying her religious services and observances. She fasted, she prayed, she interceded for the forgiveness of her sins with many tears. The

monks celebrated mass at her bed-side, and
made, as she thought, by renewing the sacrifice
of Christ, a fresh propitiation for her sins.   William, who was then in Normandy, hearing of
her forlorn and unhappy condition, came to see
her.   He arrived just in time to see her die.

They conveyed her body from the palace in
her husband's monastery at Caen to the convent
which she had built.   It was received there in
solemn state, and deposited in the tomb.   For
centuries afterward, there remained many memorials of her existence and her greatness there,
in paintings, embroideries, sacred gifts, and records, which have been gradually wasted away
by the hand of time.   They have not, however,
wholly disappeared, for travelers who visit the
spot find that many memorials and traditions
of Matilda linger there still.

William himself did not live many years after the death of his wife.   He was several years
older than she.   In fact, he was now considerably advanced in age.   He became extremely
corpulent as he grew old, which, as he was originally of a large frame, made him excessively
unwieldy.   The inconvenience resulting from
this habit of body was not the only evil that
attended it.   It affected his health, and even

threatened to end in serious if not fatal disease. While he was thus made comparatively helpless in body by the infirmities of his advancing age, he was nevertheless as active and restless in spirit as ever. It was, however, no longer the activity of youth, and hope, and progress which animated him, but rather the fitful uneasiness with which age agitates itself under the vexations which it sometimes has to endure, or struggles convulsively at the approach of real or imaginary dangers, threatening the possessions which it has been the work of life to gain. The dangers in William's case were real, not imaginary. He was continually threatened on every side. In fact, the very year before he died, the dissensions between himself and Robert broke out anew, and he was obliged, unwieldy and helpless as he was, to repair to Normandy, at the head of an armed force, to quell the disturbances which Robert and his partisans had raised.

Robert was countenanced and aided at this time by Philip, the king of France, who had always been King William's jealous and implacable rival. Philip, who, as will be recollected, was very young when William asked his aid at the time of his invasion of England, was

18

now in middle life, and at the height of his
power.   As he had refused William his aid, he
was naturally somewhat envious and jealous of
his success, and he was always ready to take
part against him.   He now aided and abetted
Robert in his turbulence and insubordination,
and ridiculed the helpless infirmities of the aged
king.

While William was in Normandy, he sub-
mitted to a course of medical treatment, in the
hope of diminishing his excessive corpulency,
and relieving the disagreeable and dangerous
symptoms which attended it.   While thus in
his physician's hands, he was, of course, confined to his chamber.   Philip, in ridicule, called
it "being in the straw."   He asked some one
who appeared at his court, having recently arrived from Normandy, whether the old woman
of England was still in the straw.   Some miserable tale-bearer, such as every where infest
society at the present day, who delight in quot-
ing to one friend what they think will excite
their anger against another, repeated these
words to William.   Sick as he was, the sar-
casm aroused him to a furious paroxysm of rage.
He swore by "God's brightness and resurrec-
tion" that, when he got out again, he would

kindle such fires in Philip's dominions, in commemoration of his delivery, as should make his realms too hot to hold him.

He kept his word—at least so far as respects the kindling of the fires; but the fires, instead of making Philip's realms too hot to hold him, by a strange yet just retribution, were simply the means of closing forever the mortal career of the hand that kindled them. The circumstances of this final scene of the great conqueror's earthly history were these:

In the execution of his threat to make Philip's dominions too hot to hold him, William, as soon as he was able to mount his horse, headed an expedition, and crossed the frontiers of Normandy, and moved forward into the heart of France, laying waste the country, as he advanced, with fire and sword. He came soon to the town of Mantes, a town upon the Seine, directly on the road to Paris. William's soldiers attacked the town with furious impetuosity, carried it by assault, and set it on fire. William followed them in, through the gates, glorying in the fulfillment of his threats of vengeance. Some timbers from a burning house had fallen into the street, and, burning there, had left a smoldering bed of embers, in which the fire was

still remaining. William, excited with the
feeling of exultation and victory, was riding
unguardedly on through the scene of ruin he
had made, issuing orders, and shouting in a
frantic manner as he went, when he was suddenly stopped by a violent recoil of his horse
from the burning embers, on which he had
stepped, and which had been concealed from
view by the ashes which covered them. William, unwieldy and comparatively helpless as
he was, was thrown with great force upon the
pommel of the saddle. He saved himself from
falling from the horse, but he immediately
found that he had sustained some serious internal injury. He was obliged to dismount, and
to be conveyed away, by a very sudden transi-
tion, from the dreadful scene of conflagration
and vengeance which he had been enacting, to
the solemn chamber of death. They made a
litter for him, and a corps of strong men was
designated to bear the heavy and now helpless
burden back to Normandy.

They took the suffering monarch to Rouen.
The ablest physicians were summoned to his
bed-side. After examining his case, they concluded that he must die. The tidings threw
the unhappy patient into a state of extreme

WILLIAM'S HORSE STEPPING ON THE EMBERS.

anxiety and terror. The recollection of the thousand deeds of selfish ambition and cruelty which he had been perpetrating, he said, all his days, filled him with remorse. He shrunk back with invincible dread from the hour, now so rapidly approaching, when he was to appear in judgment before God, and answer, like any common mortal, for his crimes. He had been accustomed all his life to consider himself as above all law, superior to all power, and beyond the reach of all judicial question. But now his time had come. He who had so often made others tremble, trembled now in his turn, with an acuteness of terror and distress which only the boldest and most high-handed offenders ever feel. He cried bitterly to God for forgiveness, and brought the monks around him to help him with incessant prayers. He ordered all the money that he had on hand to be given to the poor. He sent commands to have the churches which he had burned at Mantes rebuilt, and the other injuries which he had effected in his anger repaired. In a word, he gave himself very earnestly to the work of attempting, by all the means considered most efficacious in those days, to avert and appease the dreaded anger of heaven.

Of his three oldest sons, Robert was away; the quarrel between him and his father had become irreconcilable, and he would not come to visit him, even in his dying hours. William Rufus and Henry were there, and they remained very constantly at their father's bed-side— not, however, from a principle of filial affection, but because they wanted to be present when he should express his last wishes in respect to the disposal of his dominions. Such an expression, though oral, would be binding as a will. When, at length, the king gave his dying directions in respect to the succession, it appeared that, after all, he considered his right to the English throne as very doubtful in the sight of God. He had, in a former part of his life, promised Normandy to Robert, as his inheritance, when he himself should die; and though he had so often refused to surrender it to him while he himself continued to live, he confirmed his title to the succession now. "I have promised it to him," he said, "and I keep my promise; and yet I know that that will be a miserable country which is subject to his government. He is a proud and foolish knave, and can never prosper. As for my kingdom of England," he continued, "I bequeath it to no one, for it was not bequeathed to me. I acquired it by force, and at the price of blood. I leave it in the hands of God, only wishing that my son William Rufus may have it, for he has been submissive to me in all things." "And what do you give *me*, father?" asked Henry, eagerly, at this point. " I give you," said the king, "five thousand pounds from my treasury." "But what shall I do with my five thousand pounds," asked Henry, "if you do not give me either house or land?" "Be quiet, my son," rejoined the king, "and trust in God. Let your brothers go before you; your turn will come after theirs."

The object which had kept the young men at their father's bed-side having been now attained, they both withdrew. Henry went to get his money, and William Rufus set off immediately for England, to prepare the way for his own accession to the throne, as soon as his father should be no more.

The king determined to be removed from his castle in Rouen to a monastery which was situated at a short distance from the city, without the walls. The noise of the city disturbed him, and, besides, he thought he should feel safer to die on sacred ground. He was accordingly removed to the monastery. There, on the tenth of September, he was awakened in the morning by hearing the city bells ringing. He asked what it meant. He was told that the bells were ringing for the morning service at the church of St. Mary. He lifted up his hands, looked to heaven, and said, "I commend myself to my Lady Mary, the holy Mother of God," and almost immediately expired.

The readers of history have frequent occasion to be surprised at the sudden and total change which often takes place at the moment of the death of a mighty sovereign, and even sometimes before his death, in the indications of the respect and consideration with which his attendants and followers regard him. In William's case, as has happened in many other cases since, the moment he ceased to breathe he was utterly abandoned. Every body fled, carrying with them, as they went, whatever they could seize from the chamber—the arms, the furniture, the dresses, and the plate; for all these articles became their perquisites on the decease of their master. The almost incredible statement is made that the heartless monsters actually stripped the dead body of their sovereign, to make sure of all their dues, and left it naked on the stone floor, while they bore their prizes to a

place of safety.   The body lay in this neglected
state for many hours; for the tidings of the
great monarch's death, which was so sudden at
last, produced, as it spread, universal excitement and apprehension.   No one knew to what
changes the event would lead, what wars would
follow between the sons, or what insurrections
or rebellions might have been secretly formed,
to break out suddenly when this crisis should
have arrived.   Thus the whole community were
thrown into a state of excitement and confusion.

The monk and lay brethren of the monastery at length came in, took up the body, and
prepared it for burial.   They then brought
crosses, tapers, and censers, and began to offer
prayers and to chant requiems for the repose of
the soul of the deceased.   They sent also the
Archbishop of Rouen, to know what was to be
done with the body.   The archbishop gave orders that it should be taken to Caen, and be
deposited there in the monastery which William
had erected at the time of his marriage.

The tale which the ancient historians have
told in respect to the interment is still more extraordinary, and more inconsistent with all the
ideas we naturally form of the kind of consideration and honor which the remains of so great

a potentate would receive at the hands of his household and his officers of state, than the account of his death. It is said that all the members of his household, and all his officers, immediately after his decease, abandoned the town—all eagerly occupied in plans and maneuvers to secure their positions under the new reign. Some went in pursuit of Robert, and some to follow William Rufus. Henry locked up his money in a strong box, well ironed, and went off with it to find some place of security. There was nobody left to take the neglected body to the grave.

At last a countryman was found who undertook to transport the heavy burden from Rouen to Caen. He procured a cart, and conveyed it from the monastery to the river, where it was put on board a vessel, and taken down the Seine to its mouth, and thence by sea to Caen. The Abbot of St. Stephen's, which was the name of William's monastery there, came, with some monks and a procession of the people, to accompany the body to the abbey. As this procession was moving along, however, a fire broke out in the town, and the attendants, actuated either by a sense of duty requiring them to aid in extinguishing the flames, or by curiosity to witness the conflagration, abandoned the funeral cortège. The procession was broken up, and the whole multitude, clergy and laity, went off to the fire, leaving the coffin, with its bearers, alone. The bearers, however, went on, and conveyed their charge to the church within the abbey walls.

When the time arrived for the interment, a great company assembled to witness the ceremonies. Stones had been taken up in the church floor, and a grave dug. A stone coffin, a sort of sarcophagus, had been prepared, and placed in the grave as a receptacle for the body. When all was ready, and the body was about to be let down, a man suddenly came forward from the crowd and arrested the proceedings. He said that the land on which the abbey stood belonged to him ; that William had taken forcible possession of it, for the abbey, at the time of his marriage ; that he, the owner, had been compelled thus far to submit to this wrong, inasmuch as he had, during William's life-time, no means of redress, but now he protested against a spoliation. "The land," he said, "is mine ; it belonged to my father. I have not sold it, or forfeited it, nor pledged it, nor given it. It is my right. I claim it. In the